G000116252

DR. D. K. OLUKOYA

# Your Foundation

## and

# Your Destiny

-i-

*1st Printing* - May, 2001
DR. D. K. OLUKOYA

ISBN 978-35755-1-1

All Scripture is from the King James Version
Cover illustration: Sister Shade Olukoya

## PUBLICATIONS BY DR. D. K. OLUKOYA PUBLISHED AND MARKETED BY THE BATTLE CRY CHRISTIAN MINISTRIES

1. "Adura Agbayori" (Yoruba Version of the Second Edition of Pray Your Way to Breakthroughs).
2. "Awon Adura Ti Nsi Oke Didi" (Yoruba Prayer Book)
3. Be Prepared.
4. Breakthrough Prayers for Business Professionals.
5. Brokenness.
6. Comment Se Delivrer Soi-Meme (French Edition of How To Receive Personal Deliverance).
7. Criminals in the House of God.
8. Dealing With Unprofitable Roots.
9. Deliverance by Fire
10. Deliverance from Spirit Husband and Spirit Wife.
11. Deliverance of the Head.
12. Drawers of Power from the Heavenlies.
13. Holy Fever.
14. Holy Cry.
15. How to Obtain Personal Deliverance (Second Edition).
16. Let God Answer by Fire (Annual 70 Days Prayer and Fasting).
17. Limiting God.
18. Meat For Champions.
19. Overpowering Witchcraft.
20. Personal Spiritual Check-up.
21. POUVOIR CONTRE LESS TERRORISTES SPIRITUELLES (French Edition of Power Against Spiritual Terrorists).
22. Power Against Coffin Spirits.
23. Power Against Destiny Quenchers.
24. Power Against Dream Criminals
25. Power Against Local Wickedness.
26. Power Against Marine Spirits.
27. Power Against Spiritual Terrorists.
28. Power Must Change Hands.
29. Powerful Confessions.

## BOOKS BY OTHER AUTHORS PUBLISHED AND MARKETED BY THE BATTLE CRY CHRISTIAN MINISTRIES

### ALL OBTAINABLE AT:

☞ 11, Gbeto Street, off Iyana Church Bus Stop, Iwaya Road, Iwaya, Yaba, P. O. Box 12272, Ikeja, Lagos.

☞ 15, Olumo Street, Onike, Yaba, Lagos.

☞ 2, Oregun Road, by Radio Bus Stop, Ikeja, Lagos.

☞ MFM Prayer City, KM 12, Lagos/Ibadan Expressway.

☞ All leading Christian bookstores.

# CONTENTS

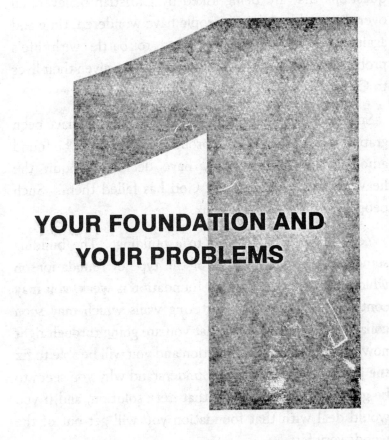

# YOUR FOUNDATION AND
# YOUR PROBLEMS

## Your Foundation and Your Destiny

*This* book will provide deep answers to many of the questions that are being asked by Christian believers all over the world. A lot of people have wondered, time and again, why they have continued to battle with life's problems in spite of the fact that they have given their lives to Christ.

Some believers have also wondered why they have been grappling with the kinds of problems that cannot be found among unbelievers. Many have decided to quit the heavenly race thinking that God has failed them. Such people need to read this book.

Your life can be likened to a building. The building stands or falls on the basis of the type of foundation on which it is erected. If your foundation is weak, you may continue to battle with tottering walls which may soon collapse. Do not look at what you are going through right now, go back to your foundation and you will be able to fix the jig-saw puzzle. You will understand why you seem to be going through problems that defy solution, and if you would deal with that foundation you will get out of the woods very fast.

There is no one without a past; we all have a foundation. Of course, your past dates back to the time of your fore-fathers or your grand-parents. Many of us live as if the past does not exist, yet you are born again; but were your ancestors born again? If your ancestors got themselves involved with ritual killings, bloody inter-tribal wars, sacrifice of new-born babies, twins and virgins to the gods of the land, then your foundation has a problem.

If anyone along your family line ever got involved with the pounding of new-born babies or other fellow human beings for use in money-making rituals, your foundation is bad. If your ancestors were idol priests or members of a masquerade cult, your foundation is demonic.

Of course, if your grand-father was a fetish priest, or if you have shrines attached to the compound of your ancestors, the building of your life has been erected on the foundation of idolatry and fetishism. Such a building cannot stand. If your maternal ancestors were priestesses and princesses of certain idols in your village, you have inherited a demonic foundation.

The problem of the African has been compounded by certain beliefs in the importance of the African culture. A lot of people mistake idolatry for culture. Any departure from things like the worship of (the god of iron), the goddess of fertility, the god of wealth, productivity, and the god of creativity would be seen as casting aspersions on African culture. This makes them resist the good news of the gospel which they regard as foreign.

This way, people ignorantly wish to hold on to ancestral worship. This can be traced the multiple spiritual and social problems plaguing many African societies today, because ancestral and idol worship form demonic foundation on which many African families are built. If such problems we have mentioned have resulted from satanic foundations, then the importance of good foundation for everything we do cannot be over-emphasised.

Isaiah 28:16:

Therefore thus saith the Lord GOD, Behold, I lay in Zion for a foundation a stone, a tried stone, a precious corner *stone*, a sure foundation: he that believeth shall not make haste.

Here is God now, wanting to plant our redemption and salvation. He first of all laid a solid foundation. The church itself is put on the foundation of the apostles and the prophets.

Psalm 11:3:

If the foundations be destroyed, what can the righteous do.

# WHAT IS FOUNDATION?

Foundation is the basis on which something depends, the basis on which it stands, the basis on which it rests.

## Your Foundation and Your Destiny

Foundation is the underground structure in a building, to support that building. When we say somebody is the founder of something, this means that person has been used to bring such a thing into existence. So, the structure below the surface of the ground which supports that particular thing is called foundation. We need to understand this very well.

The foundation is that part of the building that transfers and distributes the weight of the building according to the ground. The foundation is that upon which anything is founded, that on which it stands and that on which it rests. The stone structure or whatever it is, supports the whole structure from beneath.

The important place of the foundation, therefore, makes it a foolish thing for a builder to construct a building without a foundation or with a weak foundation.

Matthew 7:24-27:

Therefore whosoever heareth these sayings of mine, and doeth them, I will liken him unto a wise man, which built his house upon a rock: [25]And the rain descended, and the floods came, and the winds blew, and beat upon that house; and it fell not: for it was founded upon a rock. [26]And every one that heareth these sayings of mine, and doeth them not, shall be likened unto a foolish man, which built his house upon the sand: [27]And the rain descended, and the floods came, and the winds blew, and beat upon that house; and it fell: and great was the fall of it.

[11]

## Your Foundation and Your Destiny

What is the problem here? Foundation. Notice, beloved, that the rain, the flood and the winds did not discriminate in the choice of which houses to attack; they attacked both the houses but the one with the weak foundation fell.

I would like you to notice certain things about foundation. A foundation dictates the kind of structure that can be built. A foundation is hidden below; it is not conscipicious. So if you see a ministry working on foundations, like the MFM does, it is a dirty and tedious job with which the hands are soiled.

A shallow foundation carries a weak and small structure. A deep one can carry strong and giant structures. The foundation determines how durable the building is. For instance, if you grab a pupil from primary six and take him to the final class in the university for a higher degree, he is sure to have problems. The problems he will have will be foundational problems.

If you have ever been to a factory, you will have seen what is called a conveyor belt. This is designed to carry products or materials from place to place within the factory. The kind of conveyor belt you will find in a biscuit or a soap factory is not the same type you will find in a car manufacturing plant. If you place a car on a conveyor that is supposed to carry soap, it will not move.

## Your Foundation and Your Destiny

What are we trying to say here?

The point is that your life can only sustain as much prosperity as your foundation will allow. Now, the trouble is this: the foundation of many people is made up of components that are abominations to God. You cannot build a lasting prosperity upon a polluted foundation.

At MFM, we call quite a lot of prayer points that sound strange to many people. For example, when somebody says, "I command deliverance upon the foundation of my life," or "Every seed of witchcraft in my foundation, die!" People may not fully understand what the person is saying.

The problems of evil background are enormous and they have completely messed up many lives. Jesus pointed at the Jews and told them, "You are of the generation that killed the prophets." He pointed at their background.

You will be deceiving yourself, beloved, and you will be very naive to believe that your background of participation in tribal rituals, of collecting chieftaincy titles, of collecting your name from an oracle, of being born by a father who uses charms, amulets, idols and rings or being born by parents who accepted the services of demons; parents who kept slaves; parents who punished missionaries and killed them; parents who sold slaves; or parents who ground day-old babies in mortars; by being born in a polygamous set-up,

[13]

would have no effect on your life.

Leviticus 26:39:

And they that are left of you shall pine away in their iniquity in your enemies' lands; and also in the iniquities of their fathers shall they pine away with them.

And in Isaiah 65:6-7:

Behold, *it is* written before me: I will not keep silence, but will recompense, even recompense into their bosom, [7]Your iniquities, and the iniquities of your fathers together, saith the LORD, which have burned incense upon the mountains, and blasphemed me upon the hills: therefore will I measure their former work into their bosom.

Jesus referred to a particular generation as "a whole faithless generation . . ." The problem remains till today. If you are unable to believe God, the problem may be rooted in your background.

The big truth is that the full scope of evil background has neither been adequately presented to many people; nor have they comprehended these things.

Many people are saved, sanctified and filled with the Holy Spirit, but until the fire of the Holy Ghost works on the foundation of their lives they will not be able to move ahead. You need to pray today that every problem rooted in polluted foundations should give way.

Do you hear voices? Or compulsive disturbing thoughts?

Do you have problems attending church or reading the Bible? Is your sex life abnormal in any way? Is life harder for you and your problems greater now that you are a Christian than before you became one?

Do you ever see or sense some dark figures come up before you? Do you hear strange noises? Do you go into uncontrollable anger? Did you look at your daddy and find that he has a very bad temper? And now you look at yourself and see the same bad temper? And, perhaps, all your children too have that bad temper?

You need deliverance.

Do you experience a cold presence in your bed? Do you ever go into trances or black-outs and you cannot remember where you are? Do you experience continuous nightmares? Do you ever experience a loss of control?

Some people would think, think and think themselves out of faith. Are you like this? If so, you need to send fire to your foundation immediately.

# CONSEQUENCES OF BAD FOUNDATION

Bad foundation or evil background could lead to spiritual

blindness.

Evil background could lead to wild pentecostalism, whereby a person is rolling on the floor and prophesying at the same time.

All the thoughts or acts of suicide, inexplicable marital problems, bed-wetting, strange accidents, violent deaths; sexual problems, abnormal life, unrestrained anger, talkativeness, unrestrained recklessness, inner anguish, being depressed and unhappy are evidences that something is wrong with the foundation.

If you experience anyone or more of these, you need to sit up.

The Bible makes us understand that if you have a bad father you will have to do something to make your destiny come alive. Even if you have a good father, you still have to work hard.

A person who has bad parents has already started his life on a bad deficit.

Ancestral foundational bondage fertilises problems. Ancestral spirits have destroyed so many people. It is, therefore, very tragic when you are worshipping the source of your problems. It is very tragic when you go to the source of your problems to accept chieftaincy titles.

## Your Foundation and Your Destiny

Look around your family house for images, symbols, marks and totems. If you observe the presence of anyone or more of these, it is enough evidence that you need to pray fire prayer.

Many of us just look at these things without asking questions. We should be asking questions. Check your body for any mark there. Can you explain all the marks on your body? Check your legs, hands, cheeks, thighs, face, armpits and neck. Do you see any mark on these places? If there are, find out what they are for, then erase them with the blood of Jesus – cancel them. This means that the power strengthening your problem may be on your skin. All those things that people mark on their skins for decoration or beauty may be responsible for their inability to settle down with a spouse.

Look critically into your family house to see images of metals, wood, carvings, stones and pictures; now that you are born again, all these must be given attention for the purpose of rejecting them and dissociating yourself from them; you must disown them.

We once had to pray for a man with **violent anger.** At a point, the man remembered that, as a **young boy,** his parents put palm oil on a cutlass in a corner of his mother's room. So, anytime that he got angry in his childhood, his parents would go and put palm oil on the cutlass. Even now that he is an old man the anger is still there. This prevents him from holding down any job or marriage. All his children are gone and would never dare live with him, until he had to deal with that cutlass. When the cutlass was destroyed physically and spiritually, things then began to happen for him positively.

I remember another sister, who, even at the age of 40, had never experienced menstruation. She began praying foundational prayers. Then, all of a sudden, God opened her eyes and she found herself as a small baby at the back of her mother who was having a quarrel with another woman.

In the heat of the quarrel, her mother cursed that may it not be well with the baby on her back if she (the mother) failed to kill the other woman she was quarrelling with. The woman fought on but the other woman did not die. Meanwhile, the evil transaction had already happened.

Until the sister saw that vision and began to pray foundational prayers, things were never well with her. Examine your family house very well. If there are images, carvings, etc., that show links with idolatry, dissociate yourself from them. Not only that, you must pray against the spirits behind such things.

Many of us have made it a habit to visit, at every holiday

[18]

or occasion, family houses that we do not understand; this serves only to renew covenants with household witchcraft residing there.

Behold, many things have been buried and they must be destroyed spiritually – through prayers. Analyse your family house and spiritually destroy the power of darkness hanging there. Maybe, they have evil costumes, or your daddy was a hunter, or a member of the lodge, or cult member or was an idol worshipper. If there are any evil costumes there, they are enough to make all the children born there to lead a useless life. There may be musical instruments that constitute sources of problems for the whole family. Go to these items, lay your hands on them spiritually and destroy them.

There may be special plants in your family compound being treated and worshipped by the family as gods. In 1992, I was praying with a particular medical doctor who had a fantastic clinic equipped with modern equipment. This notwithstanding, the doctor only managed to get only one patient in three weeks.

Then we began with him, foundational deliverance prayers during which God showed us a tree. I asked her if she knew anything about that tree. She said yes and that, in fact, for every child born in the family her father planted a tree.

When a tree has been planted on your behalf, anytime the wind blows and sways the tree back and forth, your life automatically follows the same motion. Likewise, any day that insects come to bite the tree, the person, too, will be beaten wherever he may be. And any day that they forget to put water on the plant, poverty will catch up with the person.

This was what was happening to the doctor. So we had to plan to execute a 'spiritual coup' that will lead to the secret uprooting of the tree. For this, she travelled home, got a labourer to get the smallest tree (which belonged to her as the youngest child in the family) uprooted from the family compound. She did not want any member of the family to know that she had come home, so while the labourer went to do the job, she hid herself somewhere. The labourer finished the job in no time and brought back the evil tree to the doctor where she stayed by her car.

Immediately the tree was uprooted, the doctor's father who was sleeping in the house knew. He jumped up, ran to the front of the house but the tree was already gone. He returned to where the tree formerly stood and lamented, "So she has escaped?" After saying this for three times the old man fell down and died there by the other trees.

Some have special stones in their family. For others, it may be special rivers, special rocks, special animals, special snakes, special cows, special rodents like rats and mouse being worshipped in the family.

Take time to find out the kind of spiritual sacrifice being prescribed for your parents and grand-parents. Trace such sacrifices to the idols they worship, directly or indirectly, then destroy them with fire prayer. You may not be able to lay your physical hands on them but you can stand on a holy ground and lay your spiritual hand on them.

## YOUR PROBLEMS ARE YOUR FOUNDATIONS

What about the day you were born? And the time? The date? And the season? Find out the significance and the associated problems.

Do you know that there are evil days? Cancel them by fire. Do you have a common bad habit in your family? Are you from a royal family? Then you need royal deliverance. Check these things, confess them to the Lord, lay your physical and spiritual hands on them and destroy them.

Do your parents owe people money? Are they known to be fetish? You need to pray hard as well, because those debts they owe and refuse to pay will attract streams of curses upon the children.

## Your Foundation and Your Destiny

Now, note this, are you sure you are really the child of your father? How were you conceived? Did your mother properly marry your father? Or was the woman just selling delicacies by the roadside and she was forcibly pulled in or coaxed and put in the family way?

We have many cases of married women who get pregnant for other men and then transferred the baby to their husbands. All these things are bound to strengthen your problem if you do not understand them.

Are you from a polygamous background? This may be the foundation keeping your problem in place. You must pray very hard from now on.

Then the names you have been given – check what each of your name means. Find out why you were given those names. You may have some names that you do not know why they gave them to you. Find out the number of names you were given at birth, and why you were given them. Maybe out of the six names you were given you know only two; find out the other four and what they stand for.

How can a person bear 'Onwubiko', 'Nwankwo', 'Okonkwo', 'Nwangba', 'Njoku', 'Okoronta' (small man), 'Ogunde', 'Babatunde', 'Fasanmi' (oracle has favoured me), 'Iyabo', 'Esubiyi' (born of the devil)? All these names create problems for their bearers. Find out why that name was given to you and deal with it.

I once asked a sister why she was given a particular funny name, *'Aja'* (dog) and she replied that when she was small they used to call her *"Elemikemi"* (the possessed one). Do not assume your names are innocent names. If the names are veils, dissociate yourself physically and spiritually from them.

Find out, too, whether you have family shrines. Find out whether members of your family have any special talent or gift. Perhaps you are all wrestlers or dreamers or into divination, or drummers. Find out. What is the source of the talents? What is the source of their power?

The land on which you have your family house, have you found out whether there are problems about it? Find out the forces of darkness there. Find out what was buried in the foundation. This is because people from houses and compounds where things are buried never prosper, just like you can hardly find somebody from a family of drummers and who himself is a drummer, that prospers.

Find out the origin of any special tree growing in your family compound. If you happen to be the favourite child of your parents and your parents are witchcraft practitioners, it is possible that you yourself are a witch without knowing. In this case, your progress may be hindered.

Is there any jinx in your family? Is there a strange person who appears to bring ill-luck or misfortune to other members of the family? Dissociate yourself from that person physically and spiritually.

Are there curses on your family? Find out and break the curses.

Do you have praise songs? Find out the wordings of the praise songs. Destroy those words.

Then your complexion? Your eyes? Your weight? All these can be special identity by which satan identifies you for special problems. You may not be able to change these things physically, but you can change them spiritually.

Is there any common occupation in your family? Like carving, hunting, fishing, farming, etc. Find out the meaning of each occupation. There are names, trades and occupations allotted people who serve satan as reward. Find out.

Is there any special food that members of your family must not eat? Or is there a particular one they are always eating? Find out why they are not eating some, and why they always eat others. In some families, after child birth, the woman cannot eat certain foods. If you were born into such a place you need to pray. In some families, you cannot share an egg with another person; you must swallow it alone.

Are there festivals celebrated by your family? I am asking these questions so that you can understand the relationship between your foundation and your problems.

# WHAT ARE THE IMPLICATIONS OF BAD FOUNDATION?

☞ It fertilises problems.

☞ It will strengthen the enemy.

☞ It will be causing evil reinforcement. This can happen even after a person has received deliverance, thus making the exercise a temporary relief.

☞ It establishes progress stagnancy because the foundation that should carry it is polluted.

☞ It destroys propriety.

☞ It causes closed heavens and iron ground.

☞ It causes premature death.

When somebody with evil foundation is making progress,

it can only be an epileptic progress. He will not go very far. At the end of the day, he will find that he has not moved at all.

This is a serious matter.

Jesus spoke in Matthew 23:29-31:

Woe unto you, scribes and Pharisees, hypocrites! because ye build the tombs of the prophets, and garnish the sepulchres of the righteous, [30]And say, If we had been in the days of our fathers, we would not have been partakers with them in the blood of the prophets. [31]Wherefore ye be witnesses unto yourselves, that ye are the children of them which killed the prophets.

# YOUR STRONGHOLDS AND
# YOUR DESTINY

## Your Foundation and Your Destiny

*You* cannot fulfil your destiny in life until you begin to face certain stark realities. You have a destiny which the enemy is contesting with every vein of hatred in him. The devil knows that if every one of us were allowed to fulfil our divine destiny he would be in for trouble. This explains why he concentrates a greater percentage of his energy on destroying good destinies.

The devil is more intelligent than many of us can imagine. He does not dispute the fact that God has given you a glorious destiny; he only sets himself the task of building evil strongholds in order to destroy the good potentials inherent in your destiny. If you must fulfil your destiny you will have to allow God to dig very deep into your life and deal decisively with every satanic stronghold.

The devil is an expert at building strongholds. He is always busy building a stronghold beside every good destiny. He tries to counteract your good actions with evil reactions in order to make you earn a zero as far as your destiny is concerned.

The strongholds which the devil builds are as strong as the name suggests. He knows that as far as a stronghold is in place, it will be difficult for you to fulfil your destiny in life.

[28]

## Your Foundation and Your Destiny

The subject we are considering in this chapter is so important that you need some serious preparation so that you can get the best out of it. The devil cannot be handled with kid's gloves; he is so stubborn that your pleas and entreaties will only fall on his deaf ears. The only language he understands is the language of violence. Even if you jaw-jaw with the devil, like the people of the world say, he will not budge. He can only bow to the force of spiritual warfare.

Your destiny is so crucial that you must be prepared to fight with the last ounce of energy in your veins in order to get off the clutches of the wicked one.

There is nothing as painful as watching helplessly while the devil plunders destinies which would have made great impact in time and in eternity.

If you listen to the kind of stories that I have listened to over the years, holy violence will erupt in the volcano of your prayer altar. You will be so angry with the devil that you will vow to give him a tough fight until he takes his wicked hands off the destinies of the dear children of God.

Do you want to wrest your destiny out of satan's hands? Are you willing to experience fulfilment in every department of your life? Are you ready to say bye-bye to everything that resembles lamentations of destiny? Do you

[29]

want to get to a point where you begin to achieve the divine blueprint for your life? You have battles to do. You will win but you must fight until every foe is vanquished. You must go into several sessions of aggressive warfare prayer. Tell the devil, "You didn't create my destiny; I won't allow you to destroy it."

Go to the battle field with holy anger as we take the following preliminary prayer points

Prepare yourself with this war song:

You are the mighty man in battle,
El-Shaddai;
You are the might man in battle,
Jehovah Nissi;
You are the mighty man in battle,
Glory to Your name

1.   O Lord, let Your fire locate the foundation of my life, in the name of Jesus.

2.   Father Lord, run Your fire through every part of my life, in the name of Jesus.

3.   Father, baptise me with the anointing that cannot be defeated, in the name of Jesus;

4.   You spirits attached to demonic strongholds, built

against my life, what are you waiting for? die, in the name of Jesus;

5.   Holy Ghost, thunder, strike and destroy every satanic stronghold built against my foundation, in the name of Jesus.

6.   I cover my destiny with the blood of Jesus.

If you really handled the above prayer points with holy violence, you will have ignited confusion in the camp of the enemy. Let us go into the scriptures.

2 Cor. 10:3-4:

For though we walk in the flesh, we do not war after the flesh: 4(For the weapons of our warfare *are* not carnal, but mighty through God to the pulling down of strongholds.

The world is a battle field. Satan focuses his attack on the destinies of men and women. He knows that once he is able to destroy your destiny and has taken away the structure; what would be left is an empty shell.

The devil is fighting in order to gain control of your destiny. He wants to manipulate it so as to divest it of the glory, success and fulfilment which God has loaded into it. But the choice is yours: to allow the devil have his way or to let the will of God prevail in your life. The devil does not have the last say over your destiny.

If the devil ever has any say at all, it is an aberration. In fact, God has invested you with the power to change your destiny for good.

If the devil has had a field day destroying your life and destiny, you can decide to reverse the trend. The fact that you are already reading this book shows that God wants you to wrest your destiny out of the devil's hands.

For us in Africa, and in the third world generally, our greatest need is deliverance of our destinies. African and third world countries will attain the status of developed countries when individuals in those nations go through what I call the "deliverance of destiny."

Men and women will get into a new realm of productivity, scientific inventions, success, material and spiritual prosperity, excellence in life and ministry and a raise in their standard of living.

# THE ENEMY IN THE CAMP

The greatest source of defeat that men and women have is the enemy in the camp. The day you paralyse and neutralise the enemy in your own camp, your destiny changes for the best.

## Your Foundation and Your Destiny

There was something in a young king that offended an old king. The old king grew annoyed and sentenced the young king to death. Because it was just a little thing that started the rebellion, he had many supporters and this very fact was going to be his albatross. But, all of a sudden, the old king changed his mind and called the young king and said,

"Well, on second thought, I don't wish to kill you and if you pass my test you will live. But if you fail, you must die."

And what was the test?

The young king was to walk from the king's palace to the market with a cup of water filled to the brim and must not allow one drop to fall to the ground. On the day of the test the young king took the water from the king's palace and made his way to the marketplace. On one side of the road were some people hailing him,

"Down with the king; disobey him."

And on the other side were others pulling him down, rebuking him:

"You are not a serious person; you are a bad boy."

He carried his cup and moved on. Until he got to the market place, not a single drop of water fell from the cup.

After he had finished someone asked him:

"How were you able to succeed?"

The young fellow replied,

"I refused to listen to those who were praising me; I refused to listen to those who were insulting me. I just focussed my attention on the water."

Those people praising him and those who were criticising him were trying to appeal to the enemy in the camp of the man. If those enemies did not die, the young king would have lost his life. The old king wanted to exploit the enemy in his camp as the praises he was receiving would have made him to be puffed up, and, in the process, the water would have dropped.

Likewise, the abusive words they were raining on him would have got him angry; the anger would have made him throw off the water and he would have lost his life, if the enemy in his camp had not died.

As a student, many years back, I had a classmate. Any time that we committed any offence, the whole class would be flogged. While some of us would be rolling on the floor from the beating, this classmate of mine would stand on his feet and receive six canes without wincing.

But about an hour later, the boy would go to the toilet

and start crying there secretly. This boy was always stubborn towards the teachers, so, they too, were always prepared to deal with him. For this reason, he was always beaten more than the other students. And although he would not cry in the presence of the teachers after receiving such extra punishments, he would later retire to the toilet to cry secretly. Eventually, the boy grew very sick. There was an enemy in his camp.

# STRONGHOLDS

Apostle Paul said, "Though we walk in the flesh, we war not after the flesh: (For the weapons of our warfare are not carnal, but mighty through God to the pulling down of strongholds)."

Those things through God to the pulling down of strongholds are the same things that Jesus described as the "armour of the spirit man."

Luke 11:21-22:

When a strong man armed keepeth his palace, his goods are in peace: [22]But when a stronger than he shall come upon him, and overcome him, he taketh from him all his armour wherein he trusted, and divideth his spoils.

The armour of the strongman is the same thing that

apostle Paul described as strongholds. It is important for us to take note of this because this thing we call strongholds shall be pursued strongly so that we can flush them out of the life of everyone so that they will not have a hiding place.

The stronghold is the spiritual corner where satan and his demons hide and are protected. Every successful deliverance and spiritual warfare must begin first of all by removing whatever is defending your enemy. It is a pity that many who are involved in spiritual warfare are actively defending their enemy. Are you defending your enemy? If you have been defending your enemy, you'd better repent.

For your arrow of prayer to enter into the bosom of your enemy, your enemy's armour must be removed. When you compromise your faith and enter into iniquity, you go into bondage and you thus end up defending your enemy from the arrow of judgement. That is why many of us quote the Bible against our enemy but find out that those scriptures that we quote hardly have any effect on the enemy at all. It is because the enemy is armoured.

There is still a stronghold there where the enemy hides. And until you detect that stronghold and tear it down, life will continue to be unbearable and complete victory will remain but a dream. Are you defending your enemy? Repent.

Where exactly can we find the devil?

This is very simple: it is in darkness. Wherever there is spiritual darkness, there the devil dwells. For any lasting victory we must detect which areas of our lives where there is darkness as they are prone to the enemy attack. And when we say darkness we must understand this as an area without light.

Wherever there is disobedience to the word of God there is spiritual darkness and that place will be turned to a centre of enemy activities. The Bible says, "Take heed, lest the light in you becomes darkness." When you habour sin in your body, the light in you become darkness. Those areas you hide are darkness which shall become your areas of defeat. The secret you are hiding from the man of God is an area of future defeat. So, the real enemy of many Christians is, indeed, the internal stronghold. Therefore, before you attempt tackling satan you must ensure that the real enemy is not inside you.

Any time the devil accuses you of one wrong-doing or the other and you look inward at strategies to deal with the internal problem, you are then on the way to victory. When the devil accuses you of one sin and you know that he is right you had better make amends quickly. Whenever we discover a problem in our lives we must not excuse or defend ourselves. Doing so will only help us develop dark strong room.

In the Old Testament, a stronghold was a fortified dwelling place used as a means of protection from the enemy. Strongholds are easy to defend but difficult to attack. All the powerful, vigorously protected spiritual sins constitute strongholds.

All kinds of thinking, (thought patterns) or ideas that put people against God are strongholds.

Any kind of thinking or activity that exalts itself above the knowledge of God is a stronghold. And this stronghold is a sort of protection or defence for the devil.

Any thought of our heart that is not surrendered to Jesus is a stronghold defending the devil.

There is no power of darkness that can resist the power of the kind of prayer that we pray at the Mountain of Fire and Miracles. The most difficult problem, however, is when the Christian is defending or protecting the enemy. Our thoughts, attitudes and experiences which are in agreement with evil are defence for the enemy. We must pull down this stronghold, by repentance and warfare prayer.

These strongholds are a system of thought or an order of bondage in the mind or the body used by the devil to attack you.

A stronghold is an area over which the Christian has no control, an area of sin that has become the part of the life of the person.

A stronghold is, indeed, bondage that points at where the military is deeply entrenched.

A stronghold is not necessarily a demon; it is an area from where the demons operate.

The stronghold is an invisible structure put in place by a combination of demonic influence and human stubbornness.

Strongholds disperse light from the life of a person and invite dankness.

The stronghold is a focus of opposition; that is, the enemy entrenches itself there and attacks you from there.

The stronghold is a position in the territory that is not easily accessible.

A stronghold is normally a mystery to the outsider; people just look at it and wonder whatever is happening there.

A stronghold allows observation to be made without being observed. If the enemy is inside the stronghold, it can be observing everything you are doing but you cannot see the enemy.

A stronghold provides good opportunity for defence and security.

A stronghold is a position of power. When the enemy is inside the stronghold, he feels very comfortable.

A stronghold is a power structure, that is, in the spiritual world.

A stronghold is a focussed defiance defying you.

A stronghold is a defender of the enemy.

Once again, I ask you: Are you defending your enemy? That which the Lord has been screaming into your ears; through messages, prophecies, dreams, visions, yet you have not changed! It is a stronghold.

I am not asking you whether you go to church or not, the most important thing right now is that if there is a stronghold of the enemy in your life it will affect your destiny.

But something is wonderful: the enemy flees when the stronghold has fallen apart.

Are you ready to tear down the stronghold in your life? We can only tear it down by repentance and warfare.

There was a very brilliant boy who was constantly chased from school to school until he came for deliverance. What happened to him?

Anytime he was in the classroom, before the teacher could stop asking a question, the demon inside of him had an answer. The teachers were getting embarrassed. At times when the teacher was working mathematics on the board and makes a mistake, the demon inside the boy would talk: "Foolish teacher, this is wrong."

Sometimes, the demon would tell the teacher, "Teacher, I'm more intelligent than you are." For this, the boy was driven out of one school after the other. That was an inherited stronghold in the boy's life as his internal stronghold.

When your enemy is inside a stronghold, you have a serious problem. But you need to pull down that internal stronghold so that you can live in peace. You can fire your arrow of prayer straight at your enemy in his hiding. If he is hiding inside the stronghold, and you have not pulled it down, it will not work.

This is why so many Christians suffer defeat over and over again. To the best of their knowledge, they are doing everything right, paying their tithe, coming to church, and, by the grace of God, they are sanctified, received baptism in the Holy Spirit, yet problems plague their lives and they are struggling with the harassment of the enemy.

Are you tired of struggling? The Bible teaches that our disobedience or the disobedience of others can develop into a stronghold that can begin to pass from generation to generation, in individuals and families.

It is possible to inherit a stronghold. If you come from a family that disobeys God, that is, if despite your fervent prayer and repentance, you are still struggling, there may be a stronghold in position in your life.

And when strongholds are in place, it will keep you away from what we call abundant life in Jesus. It will hinder your prayer, block your spiritual maturity, keep you from being an effective witness unto the Lord. Then, to worsen the case, it can downgrade and destroy your destiny.

A man cannot be delivered from the flesh if there is a stronghold inside the flesh. It must be pulled down before you can have complete victory. You can cast out the devil but you cannot cast out a stronghold. Indeed, you cannot cast out a mind-set which is also a stronghold in some people's lives.

I remember that sister who phoned me from London sometime ago. She asked me to pray for her because she wanted to marry. I asked her to close her eyes and let us pray. But before we went further, she told me that whoever the partner would be must not be her pastor. Obviously, that sister had a mind-set which if not pulled down would bring a problem.

You cannot pull down a stronghold by attacking the branches. You have to go right to the foundation and attack it.

Strongholds will refuse to die for as long as you remain disobedient to the Lord. This is where the trouble lies.

The cry of the enemy is against most of us and it echoes in the words of that disciple: "Can anything good come out of his life?" Of course, the enemy knows everything about your life: your strength, weakness, interest, background, the history of yourself and of your village. The enemy knows that you have a hidden ladder in your life.

Perhaps the enemy has taken a long look at you and, from historical analysis, knows that no one has ever built a house in your family, nor achieved a position of influence. This then makes the enemy to ask you: "Who do you think you are? Trying to have a life better than the others'?"

Perhaps they have even conspired against you; perhaps the counsel of wickedness have spent sleepless nights to ensure that you do not move.

## Your Foundation and Your Destiny

At this point you must make the decision to pull down strongholds. By the time you have done this, you will expose them, pursue them, overtake them, then collect your property from them.

A young sister suddenly fell down and died. After people prayed fruitlessly for six hours to revive her, they abandoned her. Then one man approached her and asked God, "What is wrong?" And the Lord told the man, "Pray like this: I send the thunder of God upon every wedding ring on your finger, in the name of Jesus".

Immediately the brother prayed, the sister opened her eyes and thanked the brother. She said that immediately she fell down she found herself inside a river where a wedding was being conducted for her and somebody. But just as they were about to put a wedding ring on her finger, there came a voice of 'thunder', and the thunder struck the wedding ring and she came back to life.

There was a stronghold in that sister's life put up by the enemy.

Is there any stronghold in your life? Deal with it today.

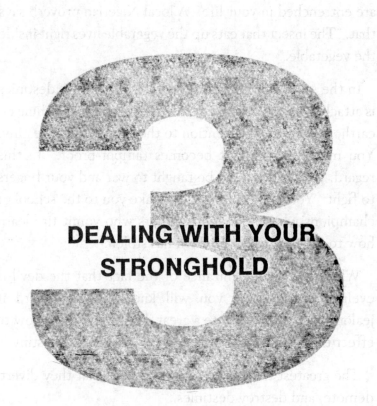

# DEALING WITH YOUR STRONGHOLD

**no** matter how great your potentials are, you cannot experience success as long as satanic strongholds are entrenched in your life. A local Nigerian proverb says that, "The insect that eats up the vegetable lives right inside the vegetable."

In the same vein, the stronghold that destroys destinies is attached to the destiny. If you must achieve anything on earth, you must pay attention to the state of your destiny. You must pray until it becomes tamper-proof. In this regard, your hands must be taught to war and your fingers to fight. You must allow God to take you to the school of champions where Christian soldiers who vomit fire learn how to retrieve what the devil has stolen.

When you take cognizance of the fact that the devil is eyeing your destiny, you will know how to guard it jealously. You will devote a great deal of energy to how to effect the resurrection of your dead virtues and destiny.

The greatest tragedy of a stronghold is that they divert, demote, and destroy destinies.

## WHAT IS YOUR DESTINY?

☞ Your destiny is God's purpose for your life.

## Your Foundation and Your Destiny

☞ Your destiny is your appointed or ordained future.

☞ Your destiny is what your God has pre-determined you to be before you were born.

☞ Your destiny is the reason why you were born.

☞ Your destiny is the expectation of heavens for your life.

☞ Your destiny is what is written in heavenly records concerning you.

☞ Your destiny is what God has in mind when He created you and allowed you to come into this world.

Anything that seeks to tamper with that destiny is not something to joke with at all because if you miss your destiny God has the right to cut you off and replace you. The enemy has a right to destroy you if you miss your destiny.

It is tragic to look at your life and discover that you have wasted it. If you have missed your destiny then your life has become a mere experiment; and life is too short to experiment with. How do you now become an overcomer? How do you deliver yourself from defending the enemy?

# DREAMS

We shall start from a very easy way. God is a good God. The Bible says, "God does nothing without telling His servants, the prophets."

In Job 33:13 we learn how to address the strongholds:

Why dost thou strive against him? for he giveth not account of any of his matters. For God speaketh once, yea twice, yet man perceiveth it not. In a dream, in a vision of the night, when deep sleep falleth uon men, in slumberings upon the bed; then he openeth the ears of men, and sealeth their instruction, that he may withdraw man from his purpose, and hide pride from man. He keepth back his soul from the pit and his life from perishing by the sword.

God is so concerned about the fulfilment of your destiny that He is constantly seeking ways of speaking to you. Unfortunately, many of us are so busy that we have no time for God.

There is a great deal of noise in the world, yet, the Holy Ghost does not scream. God still uses the still, small voice to speak to men. We go from place to place leaving no room for God in our lives. Therefore, God has no option than to speak to us through dreams.

Dreams can torment. Paul, inside the ship on the high seas, had a dream and told his co-travellers that, "the angel of the Lord whom I serve stood by me and told me that nobody shall perish." We need to know all these things so as to be able to know where we are going. God has a way of revealing these things.

# DREAMS THAT TELL OF STRONGHOLD

There are several dreams that can tell you whether you have a stronghold or not.

*If you are not dreaming at all it is very dangerous.* In the days of danger and trouble, you will have no information. It means the enemy has blinded your spirit man and soul. On the sea, Paul talked to them and because of his dream they could not perish.

When you become a weaponless warrior is when you no longer have information from your dreams. Some people belong to this category. They need to pray to God with holy madness for Him to restore their spiritual monitor which has been stolen by the enemy.

There are those who cannot recall their dream. They may know that they had a dream but because their recalling system is faulty, they are unable to remember the details of the dream. They need to pray, as the enemy may be hiding something from them.

# Your Foundation and Your Destiny

*Dreams about going back to childhood* days is a manifestation of the presence of power or retardation not wanting you to progress beyond a particular limit.

*If you dream of wearing rags or walking in the nude*, it means the enemy is trying to put poverty and embarrassment upon your life. You need to pray against the stronghold and fire your arrow at the enemy.

*If you keep dreaming of being caged or imprisoned, or being hindered*, there are forces of limitation, forces of retrogression working in your life. You need to pray against them.

*If you keep dreaming of always serving others*, this is the spirit of slavery which seeks to make the person a perpetual servant.

*If you always dream that you start something without ever completing it, whether journey, courses, projects, buildings* etc, it means you have a vagabond anointing.

*Having sex with the opposite sex in the dream* is an evidence of the presence of spirit wife or husband. This brings marital turbulence of various kinds.

*If you are always dreaming of death* it means the enemy wants to close the chapter of your life, shut down every department of your life.

[50]

## Your Foundation and Your Destiny

*When you keep seeing dead relatives* it means there is a stronghold in your family making ancestral spirits to pursue you.

*If you keep seeing tortoise or snail*, this means slow progress which makes you to struggle and struggle without any appreciable progress.

*If you are being pursued in your dream by animals or masquerades*, these are witchcraft attacks.

*If you dream of finding yourself standing by the river or swimming in it, or just standing in it*, this is an evidence that you are being attacked from the waters. Water spirits are stronger than witchcraft spirits. In fact, they are the most powerful because there is water above the earth and there is water below it; this places human beings in the middle of water forces, as well as at their mercy.

*If you dream of being abandoned*, you will find it difficult to plan for progress.

*If you dream of aborting a pregnancy*, it means that good things will keep failing in your life.

*If you keep dreaming of having accidents*, then the enemy is trying to kill you.

*If you are dreaming of drinking poison*, it means evil is

being planned against your destiny.

*If you dream of being ambushed by the enemy*, it means the enemy is planning to harm you secretly.

*If you dream of having exhausted ammunition*, it means profitless hard-work, or failure at the edge of success.

*If you are arrested in the dream*, it means your progress has been hindered.

*If you dream of seeing rotten fruits* this represents failure in the good programme that you are doing at that particular time.

*If you are having attacks by bats* this is an evidence of sorrow and calamity from the enemy.

*If you always dream of celebrating birthdays* in your dream, this is a signal of poverty against which you need to pray.

*If something has been biting you*, it means the enemy wants you to suffer loss.

*If you dream of bleeding* it means you are about to lose your virtues; you should pray to collect back your virtues.

*If you dream of having boils all over your body*, it means you are going to have an attack that will give you general discomfort.

*If you dream of seeing burglars,* you have very dangerous enemies to content with and who would not mind to harm you.

*If you are always dreaming of burial,* it means the spirit of death and horrible mistakes is after you.

*If you dream of an attack by cat,* this is a witchcraft attack;

*If you dream of cemetery,* this represents the deadness of breakthroughs and the spirit of death.

*If you dream of corpses,* this is an attack on your happiness;

*If you find that you want to run but could only manage to crawl,* it means the enemy is trying to humiliate you.

*If you find yourself crying,* it means you are going to be engulfed in a very serious trouble.

*To see a crocodile in your dream trying to attack you,* means the enemy is trying to use your closest friend to deceive you.

*When you don't use jewelries but keep seeing these on your body,* then the enemy wants to attack your destiny with gossips.

*If you see rotten eggs*, it means that, if you are not very prayerful, you will lose a lot of prosperity.

*If you are being shot in the dream*, it is a witchcraft attack against your life and your destiny.

*When you are very hungry and thirsty in your dream*, this represents the spirit of discomfort and dissatisfaction.

*If you keep seeing nails*, it means you will be doing much work but having little progress.

*If you keep seeing pepper in the dream,* it means the enemy wants to use serious punishment and victimisation against you.

*If you keep seeing cobwebs in the dream*, it means stagnancy, that is, the person's progress is being put on the shelf by the devil.

These are just some dreams problems. Should one or more of them apply to you I counsel you to pray with holy madness to cancel it out of your life. But first: you must repent. We must look into our lives to see what therein is defending the enemy.

What is the kind of thought that you think? Are evil thoughts in your life? Do you have a mind-set you do not want to change?

You have to repent. After the repentance you can see whatever problem you may be going through as opportunity in disguise or unrecognised blessings. Such problems provide opportunities for spiritual battles. You must get yourself ready at all times to do that battle, possibly by starting with this prayer to the Lord:

"O Lord, I repent for allowing strongholds in my life; I regret that I have been defending my enemies. I don't want to defend them anymore. I want Your fire to expose them so that I can possess my possessions."

You need to pray for your family too, for any stronghold that may be there to be pulled down.

Through your dream, you can know whether you have a stronghold in your life or not. When a man is fifty years old, he must have spent twenty years sleeping. Dreams occur during sleep.

These dreams form a vision during sleep. They reveal your different aims and objectives.

These dreams are spiritual monitoring system which helps you to deal with the physical. They reveal your past and your future. They can enlighten you or warn you. They are very important, so they should not be ignored.

[55]

The only dreams that could be ignored are dreams had during illness, or during moments of crisis, or the malaria induced dreams, or when you over-feed yourself.

Dreams are invisible tools; they bring messages to you from the spiritual world. That is why there are, at least, twenty-eight accounts of dreams in the Old Testament and the New Testament.

For instance, Joseph number one dreamt of eleven stars and the moon bow down for him.

Joseph number two in the Bible too, had a dream wherein an angel said, "Don't put away your wife Mary". The child she is carrying is from the Holy Spirit."

The wife of Pilate was tormented in the dream because of Jesus.

## PRAYER POINTS

1. I will make it, in the name of Jesus.

2. O God, arise and let my stronghold scatter, in the name of Jesus.

3. You the strongman in charge of my career (or any other thing it may be), I bury you today, in the name

of Jesus.

4. You the strongman in charge of my calling, die, in the name of Jesus.

5. Every ancestral strongman; die, in the name of Jesus.

6. Every witchcraft presence in my dream, what are you waiting for? die, in the name of Jesus.

7. Every stronghold mounted against my destiny, I pull you down, in the name of Jesus.

8. Every evil family pattern of family destruction, die, in the name of Jesus.

9. Every pattern of family destruction, die, in the name of Jesus.

10. Every seat of witchcraft in my roots, die, in the name of Jesus.

11. Pillar of darkness, die, in the name of Jesus.

12. Every arrow of oppression, die, in the name of Jesus.

13. Every plan of marine spirit working against my destiny, die, in the name of Jesus.

14. Every arrangement of darkness seeking my destiny, die, in the name of Jesus.

15. Every yoke developer, carry your yoke, in the name of Jesus.

16. Every padlock of darkness targeted against me, die, in the name of Jesus.

17. (Lay your hands on your head.) Anointing of open heaven descend upon my life, in the name of Jesus.

18. (Lay your hand on any ailing part of your body.) Every trace of infirmity, vanish, in the name of Jesus.

# 4

# YOUR BATTLES AND
# YOUR ANCESTORS

# INTRODUCTION

*I* believe that this is the time when God wants you to experience turn-around breakthroughs. You cannot go through this book and remain the same. No matter what you are going through, you can experience a divine change as far as your destiny is concerned. I may not know the details of what you have been through but I know that God can change your destiny.

Perhaps certain situations have been boasting or bragging against you, such situations shall be silenced, in the name of Jesus. God will manifest His power in your life, in the name of Jesus. I challenge you, at this moment, to take the following prayer points with thunder and fire in your voice:

1. Every Goliath working against my moving forward, die! In the name of Jesus.

2. I challenge my destiny with the fire of the Holy Ghost, in the name of Jesus.

3. From henceforth, I shall move forward by fire, in the name of Jesus.

4. O Lord, let this become the moment of unprecedented breakthroughs in my life, in the name of Jesus.

# THE MYSTERIES OF PROBLEMS OF LIFE

The message contained in this chapter has been specially vomited by the Holy Ghost in order to lead you to the point of turn-around breakthroughs and reverse stubborn situations in your life.

It is saddening that a lot of people grapple endlessly with stubborn problems and situations. Unfortunately, many have given up and are waiting for the worst to happen.

True to the expectations of many, things are going from bad to worse. This level trend can be traced to the fact that majority are fighting fake fires while the real issues are left unattended to.

Ignorance is a silent killer. Many are already sentenced to a grave-like existence. No wonder, our rural and urban centres are filled with walking corpses.

To worsen the situation, churches are filled with worshippers that are caged in steel coffins.

The cases of many are already finished in the spiritual realm, hence the more they struggle here on earth the more sinister forces are busy adding more nails to the coffin.

Whenever anyone around these victims volunteer any help, everything ends up in futility.

The devil, the arch-enemy of mankind takes delight in this scenario. He takes delight in perpetuating human suffering simply because he is wicked to the core. He has vowed to rob man of God's goodness, glory and blessings.

## THE RACE AND THE BATTLE OF LIFE

Against this back-drop, God has decided to take the mask off our faces in order to make us to come to terms with reality. There is no problem which God cannot solve. He can quench every evil flame and stop every evil tide from making a ship-wreck of your life. He offers a solution that goes right to the root of the problems in your life. His intention is to lay the axe of fire to every evil root that has entrenched itself in the foundation of your life.

Follow me to the scriptures as we examine the divine blue-print for receiving and experiencing God's best:

I therefore so run, not as uncertainly, so fight I, not as one that beateth the air (I Corinthians 9:26).

This passage teaches that you must observe the rules of the game if you must win in life. This accounts for the difference between success and failure, problems and promotion, victory and defeat, as well as the difference between remaining in the valley or getting to the top of the mountain.

Unfortunately, many are running the race of life on a wrong track. Such are already defeated.

Close your eyes for a moment as you take this crucial prayer point:

*I shall not fight in vain; I shall not fight to lose, in the name of Jesus.*

My heart goes after men and women who are running life's race without any destination in mind. I am also burdened for those who are engaged in purposeless fights.

It goes without saying that the enemy has converted the world in to a boxing ring. The world in which we live is an arena of tribulations. It is a tournament of trials and temptations. It is also a place where the highest form of wickedness is displayed.

The field of life is littered with casualties of war. The world has been converted into a garden of thorns and thistles. Life is, therefore, a battle. You are not doing warfare against flesh and blood; you are battling with unseen forces. It is a do or die matter. You either fight or perish.

Perhaps you are at this moment in the throes of fierce battles. Maybe the battle is getting hotter by the day.

## Your Foundation and Your Destiny

Many serious things might have been happening to you. Perhaps these things have left you confused, bewildered and perplexed. It is possible that you do not even know what to do again. Who knows, you may not know whether to live or die.

Yes, you may not know what to do but there are no questions in your mind concerning the fact that there is a vicious war going on in your life. You owe yourself the duty of putting paid to every form of evil aggression targeted against your life.

This reminds me of the story of a man who decided to deal decisively with stubborn enemies who vowed to give him no rest.

Previously, the same man had remained a victim of perpetual attacks simply because he did not know how to keep the enemies that were pestering his life at bay.

Along the line, God brought the man into one of our prayer meetings where he learnt the art, or, if you like, the science of spiritual warfare. The man happened to be a hard-working farmer but he had little or nothing to show for his efforts. Harvest time was, therefore, a time of sorrow. However, the period between the time of harvest was characterized by a peculiar feature.

A putrefying odour always greeted him whenever he got

to the precincts of his large farm. Whenever he moved closer, he often discovered that his farmland was always dotted by human excreta. This often saddened him. Anyway, he did not know what to do about the mysterious excreta. The more he ruminated on how so many balls of excreta found their ways into his farm, the more confused he became.

For a long time, he suffered the pains of bearing the burden of fruitless labour. Immediately the excreta were discharged on his farmland, his crops would dry up at an alarming rate and in a strange manner. If anything, his farm's total yield was always embarrassingly low. This gave him sleepless nights. Thus, he found a long-drawn battle with poverty and penury. He suffered not for want of hard-work and diligence. His good efforts were thwarted by satanic agents.

In the midst of his travails, a good neighbour invited him to our annual anointing service. For the first time in his life, God opened his eyes to the source of his battles. Armed with anointed oil, he travelled back to his village as a changed man. Beating his chest, he declared:

"Enough is enough! This is my last bus stop! Satanic agents can no longer frustrate my efforts!"

As soon as he got back home, he waited patiently for the

spoilers. The demonic agents, being grossly unaware of the fact that power had changed hands, waited for the appropriate time to perpetrate their wickedness, thinking that it was still business as usual. They hid under the cover of darkness and defecated on the man's farmland in order to spoil his harvest.

By the time the farmer woke up the next day, he discovered that the enemies of his progress had visited his farm. "No qualms," he told himself. "Now, I have a circuit breaker. With this anointing oil in my hand, I am going to disgrace all satanic agents."

He went ahead to anoint each mound of human excreta with the anointed oil he brought home from the service. Then tragedy struck. As if a time bomb was activated, a strange feeling of discomfort hit the bowels of the perpetrators of the wickedness. The stomach discomfort was so intense that the agents of darkness were left with no option than to show themselves up and own up to the fact that they were the ones using wicked spiritual means to tamper with the farmer's yield and productivity during harvest.

They started yelling,

"We are sorry; there are strange noises in our stomach. Our bowels are shut up. We can't empty them. Please, forgive us. We are sorry!"

The farmer looked at them as if he was bewildered. However, he knew what was happening. God was only exposing the culprits.

"What did you do," he queried them.

But they just kept saying they were sorry repeatedly. The farmer simply walked away from them saying,

"Get out of my sight if you don't know what you have done."

The people walked away not knowing what to do. Three days later, they emerged with greater discomfort. This time around, they confessed all the havocs they had perpetrated. For three days, they were not able to empty their bowels simply because the farmer had anointed their faeces. That was how he broke the yoke of poverty.

If the farmer had not known how to tackle the powers of darkness head-on, he would have remained a loser in the battle of life.

# FOUNDATION - DETERMINANT OF FAILURE AND SUCCESS IN THE BATTLE OF LIFE

The knowledge of the right approach to the battles of life is crucial. If you fight life's battles using the wrong methods, your goodness will be taken captive.

You must understand the principles of spiritual warfare.

Ignorance will lead to defeat.

You must understand the principles governing the battles of life.

You must fight in order to defend your territory.

You must fight to retrieve what the enemy has taken.

Fighters in the battle of life fall into two categories: the winners and the losers.

Your performance in the battles of life determines your destiny.

To be precise, how you fare in the battles of life is determined by your foundation.

The most difficult battle to fight in life is one which is inherited. Inherited battles are difficult to win. If you face life's battles without relating it to your ancestral foundation, you will be fighting like a blind-folded man.

Tell me, how can a blind-folded man win in a wrestling match? Of course, his chances are slim. If your battles are carried over from your ancestors, you have serious work to do.

Every man will fight his own battle. However, if your battle surpasses your strength, you need a great deal of assistance. Without divine help and the proper knowledge of spiritual warfare, you will expire as soon as your strength can no longer carry you.

Demonic powers are embodiments of wickedness. They can transfer battles from generation to generation, and from person to person. Therefore, to handle the battle of life casually is to end up being a casualty on the field of battle.

To be quite honest with you, 98% of those whose bones litter the cemeteries are casualties in the battles of life.

More importantly, poverty and sickness work hand in hand in order to reduce the ability to fight the battles of life.

You must face these two powerful forces and fight them to a standstill.

Let me make these two important statements.

## Your Foundation and Your Destiny

➥ There are only two important umpires that can stop the battles of life: either the Lord Jesus or death. Except the Lord gives you the power to fight and win the battles of life you will continue to struggle with ceaseless battles which you may never win.

➥ For the unbeliever, death does not end the battles of life: it is only the gateway to the land of continued battles. If you die without Jesus, you will begin another cycle of battles.

Let me tell you something which you must never forget: your background determines your success in the battles of life.

Unfortunately, many of our ancestors prepared platforms of failure for us before we were born. Your ancestry can pollute, defile and seriously trouble your destiny. This is made very clear in the scriptures.

Leviticus 26:37-39: And they shall fall one upon another, as it were before a sword, when none pursueth: and ye shall have no power to stand before your enemies. [38]And ye shall perish among the heathen, and the land of your enemies shall eat you up. [39]And they that are left of you shall pine away in their iniquity in your enemies' lands; and also in the iniquities of their fathers shall they pine away with them.

The passage which you have just read reveals that a great chunk of life's problems are inherited. Such problems are difficult to deal with.

[70]

## Your Foundation and Your Destiny

There is no denying the fact that our ancestors have cost us serious problems. 95% of the problems that are brought to the church can be traced to the ancestral foundations of the victims.

The problems of evil background are so enormous that they have led many to live perpetually inside demonic coffins. These problems have messed up the lives of multitude.

Jesus laid everything there during His earthly Ministry by pointing accusing fingers at the ancestral foundation of the Jews. This is recorded in Matthew 23:29-35.

Woe unto you, scribes and Pharisees, hypocrites! because ye build the tombs of the prophets, and garnish the sepulchres of the righteous, <sup>30</sup>And say, If we had been in the days of our fathers, we would not have been partakers with them in the blood of the prophets. <sup>31</sup>Wherefore ye be witnesses unto yourselves, that ye are the children of them which killed the prophets. <sup>32</sup>Fill ye up then the measure of your fathers. <sup>33</sup>Ye serpents, *ye* generation of vipers, how can ye escape the damnation of hell? <sup>34</sup>Wherefore, behold, I send unto you prophets, and wise men, and scribes: and *some* of them ye shall kill and crucify; and *some* of them shall ye scourge in your synagogues, and persecute *them* from city to city: <sup>35</sup>That upon you may come all the righteous blood shed upon the earth, from the blood of righteous Abel unto the blood of Zacharias son of Barachias, whom ye slew between the temple and the altar.

The words of Jesus leave no one in doubt as regards the fact that our forefathers would have introduced serious battles into our lives.

Beloved, let me say this again as a matter of emphasis.

You would be deceiving yourself to think that participation in tribal rituals, communal sacrifices, obtaining your name through divination or consultation of oracles, having parents who use charms, amulets and other fetish materials, being linked with parents that constantly employ the services of demons, being born by parents that used slaves despitefully and wickedly and having ancestors who used human blood in certain sacrifices would leave no consequences upon your life.

These things cannot but affect your destiny. The Bible makes it crystal clear that those who come from idolatrous background will experience serious problems. Now is the time to stand against all forms of ancestral bondage.

All battles emanating from your ancestral lineage must be fought and won.

As long as these problems remain unsolved your life would be tossed back and forth like a useless coin.

# SALIENT QUESTIONS

Let me ask you these salient questions:

- Do you sometimes hear strange voices?

- Do you experience mysterious problems in your spiritual lives?

- Are you a believer and you find it difficult to pray and read the Bible?

- Do you have strange dreams?

- Are there strange marks on your body?

- Do you feel as if some unseen strange creatures are working all over your body?

- Have you noticed certain abnormal features in your life?

- Are you a strange fellow?

- Do you see what others do not see?

- Do you know things mysteriously before they happen?

- Have you surrendered yourself to Jesus and noticed that things are getting harder?

- Do you see strange figures or dark shadow?

- Do you feel the touch of invisible hands?

[73]

- Do you smell unpleasant odors?

- Do you hear strange noises when everywhere is silent?

- Do you go into fits of uncontrollable anger?

- Do you experience night mares?

- Do you often feel pressed down by invisible creatures?

- Do you sometimes experience mental blackouts?

- Do you experience fearful and disturbing night mares that leave marks on your bodies when you wake up the next day?

- Have you failed and gone through deliverance without noticeable changes in your situation?

- Do you experience mysterious problems which you find difficult to share with others?

- Have you suddenly discovered that your life has become a mixed-bag of complicated problems?

- Do you struggle endlessly to stop habits which have become a feature of your ancestral genes?

If you will decide to provide sincere answers to the questions raised above, you will discover that you have lots of battles to do against powers behind ancestral problems.

But if you continue to hide these features you will further compound your problems.

These evil backgrounds can lead to spiritual blindness. You will no longer hear the voice of God when you pray. These problems could even lead to thoughts and acts of suicide.

Marital problems could also develop as a result of these pointers to ancestral foundational bondage.

Violent death and strange accidents are also possibilities.

Abnormal or aberrant behavioural patterns could also come-up.

Other indexes or foundations or generational problems include continuous business failure, abnormal sexual urges, addiction to drugs prescribed by medical doctors, self inflicted injuries, feeling of being caged and other mysterious problems.

You must never sweep any of these under the carpet. Accept the diagnosis of the Holy Spirit and seek the face of God for total deliverance.

## RESEARCH WORK

## Your Foundation and Your Destiny

Let me share with you at this juncture the staggering details of a research that was meticulously conducted.

We started this research over thirty years ago. We made use of deliverance questionnaire forms that were used over a thirty-year period, we also questioned candidates that had undergone deliverance for over thirty years. Our opinion pole also covered general Christians including those who do not believe in the theory and practice of deliverance. At the end, we came up with the following findings.

➡ Those whose ancestors were idol worshippers generally ended up with spiritual bondage frustration and poverty.

➡ Those whose ancestors were involved with the masquerade cult generally battle with stagnancy and at the end are sentenced to a vicious circle of endless vanity.

➡ Those who come from polygamous homes suffer one form of marital distress or the other and their wives are also characterized by general backwardness.

➡ Those whose ancestors were herbalists generally operate as if they are caged. They always experience constant attacks.

➡ Those who come from riverine areas and are

offsprings of parents who were offering sacrifices to marine powers would always dream of bodies of waters. Demons will come from the marine kingdom to attack such people, their goodness are hidden under the water.

➡ Those whose parent were into the slave trade would always end up living hard lives. Members of such families suffer from untimely death because as those slaves were captured from their places of residence and loaded into the ship, they rain curses on their captors. If your father was involved in that kind of evil practice you would live under a curse, the only way out is deliverance. Do not be surprised if hardship, untimely death and poverty is prevalent in your family.

➡ Those whose ancestors were into occultic practices would suffer from diverted destinies or profitless hardwork.

➡ Those whose ancestors were thieves would suffer from incurable diseases and experience constant losses.

➡ Those whose ancestors were bastards or products of illegitimate marriages suffer from instability, unprofitable lives, spiritual blindness and non

[77]

achievement. The lives of such offsprings are placed on the shelves as abandoned projects. They will not ever achieve anything until they go to the grave.

➡ The offsprings of ancestors who led deceptive lives, would always find it difficult to make progress in life. Progress would always become aborted at the edge of success.

➡ Those whose ancestors were wicked would always experience constant witchcraft attacks.

➡ Those whose ancestors were local hunters would end-up fishing and catching nothing in life.

➡ Those whose ancestors were drummers would battle with poverty throughout their entire existence.

➡ Those whose ancestors were from royal families would be bombarded by forces of frustration and affliction.

➡ Those whose ancestors practised incest would experience marital failure and poverty.

➡ Those whose ancestors were diviners would suffer sicknesses and stagnancy.

➡ Those whose ancestors were palm wine tappers would suffer poverty and academic dullness.

## Your Foundation and Your Destiny

- Those whose parents or ancestors were trading in alcohol and cigarettes would experience constant harassment from every wicked spirit.

- Those who are raised from the family of town criers will experience lots of turbulence in life.

- Those whose ancestors spent their lives going after concubines would experience slippery and unstable relationships.

- Those whose ancestors participate in tribal or traditional dancing would experience a vagrant or vagabond lifestyle.

- Those whose ancestors were hostile to missionaries or killed preachers of the gospel would experience general blockage in life.

- Those whose ancestors practised ritual killings would suffer untimely death and instability.

- Those whose ancestors were adulterers and adulteresses would suffer marital instability and chronic diseases.

- Those whose ancestors were fond of grabbing other peoples land would suffer general backwardness in life.

# Your Foundation and Your Destiny

➤ Those whose ancestors were fake religious prophets, would experience downward pools each time efforts are made to rise-up.

➤ Those whose ancestors took part in the oppression of widows, the down-trodden and strangers would not escape the biting pangs of extreme poverty.

➤ Those whose ancestors accepted bribery in order to condemn the innocent would experience failure at the edge of breakthroughs.

➤ Those whose ancestors were witches and wizards would experience constant harassment from powers of darkness.

➤ Those whose ancestors were highly fetish would discover that nothing would work for them.

➤ Those whose ancestors were doing the work of the Lord deceitfully would experience shame, ridicule and disgrace.

➤ Those whose ancestors were murderers would sooner or latter become pursued by the blood of the slain innocent souls.

➤ Those whose ancestors were kidnappers would suffer unexplainable loss of children in their own families.

➡ Those whose ancestors engaged in doing all sorts of terrible things to other peoples' life, would be pursued by the spirit of death.

➡ Those whose ancestors were consulting the dead would live like corpses.

➡ Those whose ancestors had answered occultic or demonic names would be harassed by the spirit of failure.

The findings above have been carried out over a thirty-year period. A writer says, "Every man is a quotation of all his ancestors."

In other words, you are a product of your ancestors. There is really nothing you can do about your foundation.

However, I have good news for you. Jesus is the only one who can destroy the evil platform built by your ancestors and lead you to a new beginning.

The platform built by our ancestors is a serious problem that requires violence.

# STEPS TO TOTAL DELIVERANCE

What then, are the steps to total deliverance and freedom

from all forms of ancestral bondage and freedom?

*Confess your sins.*

*Confess the sins of your ancestors and repent on their behalf.*

*Renounce all the evil activities perpetrated by your ancestors.*

*Destroy every evil foundation.*

*Build a new foundation.*

*Build up your life afresh and align yourself with the Lord Jesus.*

This kind of message requires a great deal of praying. Many lives are already fragmented, serious spiritual warfare efforts must be carried out in order to gather the piece that has fallen apart.

The prayer point at the end of this chapter may appear strange but you need them, if your ancestors have built evil platforms under the building of your life, they must be broken today.

I counsel you to pray aggressively and to encourage you to do this I would share a brief testimony with you.

A sister suddenly discovered the presence of two organs

in her body. Initially she was born with a female reproductive organ. As soon as someone came to ask for her hand in marriage, a male organ suddenly grew out from no where. This made her to come for deliverance prayers.

As we prayed for her, we made a discovery. It was not her father who made her mother pregnant, it was a spirit husband (a demonic personality). That was the source of her problems. Do you know that many people are carriers of five-hundred-year-old ancestral bondage? If you are one of such people, would five minutes prayer get rid of such?

There is a department in the kingdom of darkness called the department of ancestral bondage.

The demons attached to that department are defiant. They do not want anyone to destroy what they have spent years erecting.

At this moment, I want you to recall activities of your ancestors. Can you remember any of their sins? Seek the face of the Lord on their behalf and ask for forgiveness.

Having discovered that your ancestral background goes a long way in affecting your life and destiny, you must spare no efforts in dealing with your past.

You need to take a thorough look at the history of your ancestral lineage and deal with any form of foundational problems accruing there.

If you disregard this point, you will be guilty of scratching your problems on the surface. Your case will then be likened to that of a man's who busies himself with the full time efforts of cutting the leaves while the roots remain firmly enriched in the soil.

# WAY OUT

What then must you do to deal with problems emanating from your ancestry. You need to do a kind of personal research into the history of the family into which you were born. To do this, you need to utilize the play back button of the video of your life.

Examine all the area where the enemy has cheated you. Take note of all the grounds which you have lost to the enemy and pinpoint all your possessions that has slipped off your fingers. Take an incisive look at the goings-on in your family line.

Recognise all the troubled spots. Take note of all recurrent evil features and identity the stubborn problems that have continued to run like an evil thread across the family line.

Take your discovery to the Lord in prayer. Ask God to intervene and bring you out of every evil family pit. Ask God to release his fire upon you ancestral foundation.

Bring your ancestral problems face to face with the power of God. The battle against ancestral foundational problems is one that your attitude to the prayer battle against stubborn ancestral problems will determine whether you will win or lose.

I encourage you to put the totality of your strength into the warfare prayer section below. Pray aggressively. Your survival depends on it. Pray like a wounded lion. Tell the devil, "Enough is enough." You will never remain the same.

# PRAYER POINTS

1. **Every foundational witchcraft** in my family, die, in the name of Jesus.

2. Every serpent in my foundation, what are you waiting for? die, in the name of Jesus.

3. Every seed of poverty in my foundation, die, in the name of Jesus.

4. Every foundational padlock, die, in the name of Jesus.

# Your Foundation and Your Destiny

5. Foundational curses, break, by the blood of Jesus.

6. Foundational evil covenants, break, by the blood of Jesus, in the name of Jesus.

7. I oppose every opposition, I pursue every pursuer, I oppress every oppressor, in the name of Jesus.

8. Every wickedness attached to my family line, die, in the name of Jesus.

9. Every foundational marine power, die, in the name of Jesus.

10. Every idol in my foundation, receive the consuming fire of God, in the name of Jesus.

11. Every power that vowed to die before I make it, die, in the name of Jesus.

Lay one hand on your head and the other hand on your stomach as you take this prayer point.

12. Dream poison, come out now, in the name of Jesus.

13. Every ancestral transmission of affliction, die, in the name of Jesus.

14. Every ancestral evil pattern, break, in the name of Jesus.

15. Firing squad, shoot down every evil bird flying against my destiny, in the name of Jesus.

[86]

# 5

**VOICES AND DESTINY**

And he came thither unto a cave, and lodged there; and, behold, the word of the Lord came to him, and he said unto him, What doest thou here, Elijah? [10]And he said, I have been very jealous for the Lord God of hosts: for the children of Israel have forsaken thy covenant, thrown down thine altars, and slain thy prophets with the sword; and I, even I only, am left; and they seek my life, to take it away. [11]And he said, Go forth, and stand upon the mount before the Lord. And, behold, the Lord passed by, and a great and strong wind rent the mountains, and brake in pieces the rocks before the Lord; but the Lord was not in the wind: and after the wind an earthquake; but the Lord was not in the earthquake: [12]And after the earthquake a fire; but the Lord was not in the fire: and after the fire a still small voice. [13]And it was so, when Elijah heard it, that he wrapped his face in his mantle, and went out, and stood in the entering in of the cave. And, behold, there came a voice unto him, and said, What doest thou here, Elijah? (1 Kings 19:9-13).

# VOICES

*Every* day we are bombarded with sounds of voices. All voices are in two categories: there is the external one and there is internal one. You cannot avoid hearing voices, but we can avoid hearing the wrong ones. We can decide not to listen to some voices and decide not to follow their instructions. God has given us this power of choice.

It may sometimes be very difficult but we can do it. That is why God has made man in His own image and put under his control things and circumstances around him. It is for this reason that a man of God once said that you may not be able to prevent a bird from flying around your home but when it wants to land on your head and defecate there, there is something you can do: you fold your wrist very well and give it a good blow.

# THE EVIL VOICE

Within the last few months, two strange incidents happened. Of course, people find it hard believing most of the experiences I share with them. A particular woman attends our church though the rest of her family worships elsewhere.

One day, while in her shop, a voice came to her telling her to go home. The voice was very strong so the woman eventually closed her shop and headed home. When she got home she found her husband and her first daughter committing immorality! She broke down and cried.

Later, daddy and daughter held a meeting and decided to deal with mummy. The woman was barred from the kitchen and her daughter assumed the duty of cooking for her father, thus making the woman an outcast in her own home.

After she told me the story, I asked her what she wanted me to do. She said she needed prayer so I gave her some prayer points. I also asked her to give me the telephone number of their house so I could speak with the daughter. She obliged.

When I called, as God would have it, it was the daughter herself that picked up the phone.

"How are you?" I greeted her.

She asked who was speaking and I mentioned my name. Immediately she heard my name there was dead silence. I asked if she was still there and she said yes. I said I would like to meet her and she asked why. I said she should just come. And she came.

When she came into my office I pointedly asked her,

"Why did you do this abomination?"

The girl broke down and wept, then said, "One voice told me to do it."

Sometime ago, a pastor had a gun in his house with which he protected himself from the menace of armed robbers tormenting residents in his area. One night, the armed robbers came calling. The pastor woke up in a jiffy and monitored the robbers' movement through his window. When the robbers got within his firing range he pulled the trigger and managed to get one of them down. The other robbers took to their heels.

He thereafter called the police to report the incident. when the police came he went out to meet them and gave them the detail of what transpired. While he did this, the robber he had gunned down was lying face down. When the policemen eventually turned the face of the slain robber up the pastor found it was his own first son!

What happened to that boy? He listened to strange voices.

When we begin to follow Jesus, many voices will start bombarding us with the sole aim of leading us astray and taking us out of sound doctrine. They want to take you away from that which God wants to plant in your life. The voices would be very loud but, more often, God speaks quietly. God does not speak while man is speaking.

## VOICES AND DESTINY

We are surrounded by so many voices and the voices that we obey determine our destiny. These days, we have a lot of people who shout, "Thus saith the Lord, thus saith the Lord," and when you look at this fellow, you will discover he is a fornicator, or a thief.

The voice we obey determines our destiny. If you listen to the voice of your manufacturer, you will do well. But immediately you start listening to the voice of the stranger, and fail to deal with the stranger the way the Bible tells you to deal with him, you will begin to get into trouble, serious trouble.

# WHOSE VOICE DO YOU OBEY?

Judas heard satan's voice and betrayed Jesus. And what happened to him? He perished. It was because of Judas that this particular statement came out of the mouth of Jesus, "The son of man goeth as it is written of him, but woe unto him that betrayed the Son of man; it would have been better if he was not born." Jesus tried to help Judas when each of His disciples wanted to know who the betrayer would be. When it came to the turn of Judas, Jesus said, "That which thou doeth, do it quickly." This was enough warning for somebody who was not listening to strange voices to run.

There was a time Peter was listening to the voice of satan. Jesus had to rebuke him.

The high priest heard satan's voice and believed it and went before Pilate to accuse Jesus.

## Your Foundation and Your Destiny

The question is: whose voice do you hear?

Pontius Pilate had decided to let Jesus go but the unrelenting voices of people made him do otherwise.

Whose voice do you follow?

One way or the other, you must be listening to some voices but where do the voices come from?

Satan is busy attacking many people from the inside. A lot of people have a noisy internal. The noise from the inside is louder than the one on the outside. When a lot of such people come for deliverance they mention this inside noise. It is satan speaking from inside such people and confusing them, urging them to do one terrible thing or the other. All these voices are false voices from the bottom of the pit.

Whose voice do you hear? Is it the voice of the truth or the voice of deceit?

A lot of people love deception.

I was once in Port Harcourt where someone requested me to pray for him. After I had prayed, I opened my eyes and saw that from her kneeling position, the woman was looking straight into my eyes. After the prayer, the woman asked me,

"What did you see?"

I asked her what she meant by this and the woman replied,

"But you must have seen something."

I replied that, well, I saw her! The woman was obviously waiting to be deceived. A lot of people like deception – always wanting people to prophesy to them, not knowing that it is not all the time that God speaks. God is not talkative. Because a lot of people have developed itchy ears, they end up listening to the voice of the enemy. As such people go from one prophet to another to hear something said about their lives and get things stolen from their lives. Some of these 'prophets' who can tell the truth do tell the truth alright.

Someone once came to me for prayers. He said he had met several satanic priests who told him the truth concerning an aspect of his life: that he, the inquirer, belonged to the camp of the Lord, so he (the priest) would not be able to help him, and that the only person who could help him was the God of the Bible.

The priest said further that when the inquirer was born, his parents dedicated him to the God of the Bible and, as such, the fellow should go no further round any prophet's place as this could result in untimely death for him.

[94]

## Your Foundation and Your Destiny

"Go back to the God of the Bible," the priest advised him.

God only wanted to help that fellow. In most situations, such priests rarely tell the truth. Even when they see clearly into a person's life by reading the palms, they twist the facts of the fellow's life. Still, the person thanks them and accepts whatever satanic verdict has been passed on him/her.

Whose voice do you obey? Do you listen to the voice of the desires of your heart or the voice of God and His words? Which is the voice that thunders in your life?

> Verily, verily, I say unto you, He that entereth not by the door into the sheepfold, but climbeth up some other way, the same is a thief and a robber. [2]But he that entereth in by the door is the shepherd of the sheep. [3]To him the porter openeth; and the sheep hear his voice: and he calleth his own sheep by name, and leadeth them out. [4]And when he putteth forth his own sheep, he goeth before them, and the sheep follow him: for they know his voice. [5]And a stranger will they not follow, but will flee from him: for they know not the voice of strangers. (John 10:1-5).

Two voices are portrayed in the above passage; the voice of the shepherd, who is Jesus. The other voice is that of satan's. When we talk of the voice of the shepherd, we are talking of the voice of God, the voice of Jesus and the voice of the Holy Spirit. To follow the voice of Jesus is to follow the voice of God and the Holy Spirit. To follow any other voice is to follow the voice of the stranger.

Your body may be making noise, you dare not listen to its voice. It is the voice of the flesh and the worldliness around us. Even the earth that we tread upon has its own voice. Likewise, trees have voices with which they speak. When you always have a giant cat crying by your window, it is saying something to you.

I once shared something at the Prayer Rain about a professor friend of mine. I used to preach to him to accept Christ. He used to laugh at me,

"You a whole doctor of molecular genetics preaching Jesus instead of breaking new grounds in genetics."

Then, something happened. He bought a brand new car. One day, by the side of the car, he heard a voice. The voice sounded strange, so he jumped out of his bed together with his wife and both of them rushed to the car garage where they saw a cat standing on its two legs like a human being. The man tried to scare the cat away but the animal did not move.

Trembling with fear, he went inside for a cutlass. Even while armed with the cutlass he was still afraid. With every courage he could summon, he threw the cutlass at the cat but the cat simply stepped aside. The cutlass entered the earth and the cat disappeared. My friend ran to Lagos to see me.

The voice coming from that cat was only sending a message into that environment. All those cries in the night are voices programmed into our environment.

When demons speak in tongues, they are only cursing you; so you must stand against it. It is not enough to bind cats, evil birds and evil voices. The voice that has entered must also be canceled. This needs to be clearly understood. We need to be careful and be able to discern in the spirit.

Which voice sounds louder to you?

Which voice do you follow? Is it the voice of your flesh or the voice of God?

Sometime ago, when I was preparing to minister somewhere, I heard the voice of the Holy Spirit telling me that a baby would be brought from somewhere for me to pray for and that the baby was not an ordinary baby. Indeed, immediately after we finished the service, the baby was brought to me. She was said to be convulsing. A lot of things had been loaded into that baby with satanic power.

At any rate, I took the baby and started to pray. All of a sudden, the baby that was lying almost lifeless in my hands had sufficient power to lift up a hand to rub my face. It now dawned on me that, this indeed, was the baby the Holy Spirit had warned me about. After I left the place, trouble began. Mother and child got into a duel and the mother began confessing to witchcraft: how she had loaded the baby in order to use her to attack the man of God. She said she heard a voice that warned her of my coming!

Which is louder in your ears?

Is it the voice of desire for pleasure, or the voice of God? Have you not read in the scriptures that those who love pleasure more than God shall be punished?

Which voice sounds louder in your ears?

Is it the voice of the lust of the eyes? Has fornication filled your heart that all you ever hear from within you is that voice ever urging you to go on fornicating?

Which voice is louder in your life?

Is it the voice of laziness that keeps you from reading your Bible and praying?

Which voice is louder in your life?

Is it the voice of wanting to talk too much or the voice of God?

Which voice is louder in your life?

Is it the voice of repeating yourself over and over or the voice of God?

Which is louder in your life?

Is it the voice of wanting everybody to like you or the voice of God?

Which voice is louder in your life?

Is it the voice of fear or the voice of God? Some people are ever afraid of many things – lack of marriage, lack of job – and every day they wake up, they have fear coming to take over their lives. Then the enemy begins to speak.

Which voice is louder in your life?

Is it the voice of anger or the voice of God? Is it the voice of wrong thinking or the voice of God?

Which voice is louder in your life?

Is it the voice of your circumstances that do not look friendly at all, making you feel that your whole world is about to collapse?

Which voice is louder in your life?

Is it the voice of bitterness, envy, jealousy or gluttony?

The Bible talks about the voice of the enemy in Psalm 55:3:

Because of the voice of the enemy, because of the oppression of the wicked: for they cast iniquity upon me, and in wrath they hate me.

Which voice is louder in your life?

Is it the voice of the enemy or the voice of the Holy Spirit? Is it that voice that says, "It is I, be not afraid," or that voice that asks you how you hope to survive that same affliction that has eaten up the lives of so many others? Do you want to listen to that voice? Or you want to listen to the voice of God?

"I know my sheep, and my sheep know my voice, and the stranger they will not follow."

# DISCERNMENT - A PRIORITY

There is one thing we need to pray for. The Bible calls it discernment. In these last days we really need to pray for discernment. We need to be able to get to a level where, immediately a person begins to talk, we can know whether he is of God or of the devil. Where, immediately we pick up a book and after reading a few sentences, we are able to discern if it is of God or the devil. We need this kind of discernment.

What is discernment?

It is the ability to ascertain whether a certain thing is from God, man or satan. It is for this reason that the Bible tells us to "test the spirits" and it also says that "By their fruit we shall know them." When somebody comes on the television screen and introduces himself as "Senior Apostle . . ." with twenty-two wives and have just married an additional ten so that his power can increase, of course, we can know that, that kind of voice is not from the Bible, because the Lord of the Bible stipulates one wife for one man. He says two shall become one, and not three or more.

It was in this ungodly fashion that one "Jesus of Oyingbo" referred to himself as the Holy Spirit in 1964, and that he would never die. The man is dead now.

Another "Jesus of Agege" predicted that Lagos would sink in 1940 but the city of Lagos is still standing. I learnt, although this is still subject to confirmation, that the man later got born again – "Jesus of Agege", giving his life to Jesus the Almighty!

Now what about all the people these people had deceived? They are finished unless they plug into Jesus. That is why it is dangerous for you to joke with your life. If witches can kill a person and drink his blood dry you need to renew your prayer power not to fall a victim. It is possible for a witch to accept Christ and get born again.

The mystery of our faith is that such a witch will be forgiven by God and allowed to go to heaven. But what about the person who had allowed his blood to be sucked by the witch until he died? He is already languishing in hell! Even when he sees the former witch enter into heaven and raises up his voice in protest against the "injustice" he is certain to win no sympathy.

This is one reason we must not joke with or make fun of our lives but always be fervent in prayer so as to be able to return evil arrows back to senders.

Discernment is the ability to discriminate between what is of God and what is of satan.

Discernment will enable you to unmask the trick of satan.

Sometime ago a man went to a village near Ile Ife to pray because he had a problem. He prayed at the top of his voice saying, "Olugboun" (the one that hears voices) "hear the voice of your son!"

After a while the man got up to go home. As he made to go, something told a brother standing close to him,

"This man who has just finished praying, did you for once hear the name of Jesus in his prayer?"

The brother was not sure he ever heard the man mention

[102]

Jesus. So he accosted the man who had just prayed and politely told him that if he did not mind he would like him to go over the prayer with him again. As courteously as he could, he told the man that, this time around, he should pray in the name of Jesus. This only attracted a buff from the man. It was then it occurred to the brother that the "Olugboun" that the man was calling was a demon inside his bedroom.

We need discernment to detect false teachers, to spot the fake before others can spot them, and the only way to have discernment is by being in touch with the Holy Spirit. We have to graduate to that level where we shall see more than human beings in whoever stands before us. We must know where they belong .

A brother once opened a factory and wanted to employ staff. On the day he was to conduct the interview, he prayed seriously.

When the first candidate entered his office and sat down, God opened the brother's eyes and told him that the person sitting before him was a cobra. He simply dismissed the person and promised to get in touch with him later.

Then the second person came in. As this one started speaking saliva started running from his mouth, whereupon the Lord told the brother that this one was an evil spirit.

Likewise, he dismissed him. The brother needed to fill six vacancies but he could only get one. He decided to conduct another interview.

We need to pray to attain this level of discernment.

Satanic agents can be despatched to your business or other institutions to disturb it. You and I need to pray to the Lord that our ears should be deaf to anti-destiny voices, that those voices speaking failure should dry up.

The voice you listen to determines your destiny. Indeed, you are reading this book now because of the voice you listened to.

Just recently someone wrote a letter to me to say that her father and mother and other siblings had run mad and had all been taken to the psychiatric hospital. She was the only one remaining sane. Even then, as she walked in the streets these days, a voice was always urging her to pull off her blouse and scaff and her wrapper and throw them off!

Which voice do you listen to?

If you listen to demonic voices, you will have your destiny altered. You must pray until all negative voices are destroyed by fire.

# PRAYER POINTS

1. O Lord, at this moment, let Your power work on my behalf, in the name of Jesus.

2. O God of heaven, perfect everything that concerns me, in the name of Jesus.

3. Every voice of the night programmed against my destiny, come out and die now, in the name of Jesus.

4. You voice of witchcraft speaking against my breakthrough, I bury you today, in the name of Jesus.

5. Every voice of household wickedness, die, in the name of Jesus.

6. Every voice of unfriendly friends, die, in the name of Jesus.

7. Every voice of failure, die, in the name of Jesus.

8. Every voice of uncertainty, die, in the name of Jesus.

9. Every voice of evil broadcasters, what are you waiting for? die! in the name of Jesus.

10. Every voice of collective captivity, die, in the name of Jesus.

11. Every voice of bewitchment, die, in the name of Jesus.

[105]

12. My destiny, be delivered from the voices of evil forces, in the name of Jesus.

13. As the Lord lives and His Spirit is alive, from this moment, all my prophets of Baal shall die and I shall defeat them on Mount Carmel; their evil voices shall not work against me, in the name of Jesus.

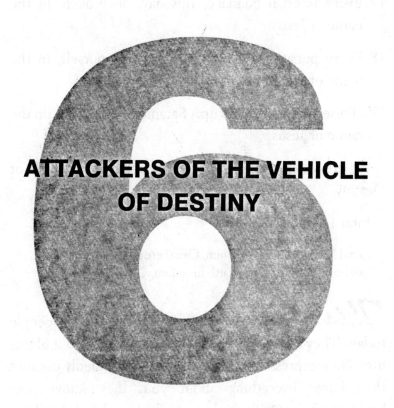

# ATTACKERS OF THE VEHICLE
# OF DESTINY

I want you to pray these prayer points before you continue.

16. O Lord, upgrade my power in the name of Jesus.

17. Every internal bondage, this day, be broken, in the name of Jesus.

18. Every pursuer in the dream, pursue yourself, in the name of Jesus.

19. (Raise your two hands up.) Satanic anchor, roast, in the name of Jesus.

We are looking at what I call, "Attacking the vehicle of Destiny."

John 1:46:

> And Nathanael said unto him, Can there any good thing come out of Nazareth? Philip saith unto him, Come and see.

*This* is the cry of the enemy against a lot of people today. They are saying, can any thing good come out of this life? They express this either verbally or impliedly because they know everything about you; they know your background; your village's history; the founder of the place; your mother and everything; therefore, they conclude, "Can any good thing come out of this person?"

[108]

# HOUSEHOLD ENEMIES

There was a brother who wedded many years ago. After the wedding, he went with his newly wedded wife to spend the honeymoon in his village, so they moved into the best room they could get there. The room also had a security gate. But around 1:00 a.m. in the night, the brother woke up to discover that somebody had opened the gate and was hearing sound of footsteps coming toward their room. He opened the window in a bid to peep at the fellow but he became glued to the bed!

At the movement of the evil personality, there was dead silence as the noise of frogs, crickets and other animals ceased. Then it dawned on the brother that trouble was around the corner, as the footsteps were approaching their room, he attempted to call the name of Jesus but he found it difficult as he felt his lips were as heavy as iron, then he started calling Jesus in his spirit. Later, the movement stopped by the window and finally went back and closed the gate. Thereafter, he woke up the wife, packed their things and ran away before 5:00 a.m.

However, the damage had been done. I pray that God would help those who are fond of their villages. Not that you go there for the sake of the gospel but to socialise and talk with palm wine drinkers. Eventually, the next menstruation of the wife had no blood, it was rather filled with maggots! By the second month it was the same thing. She went to the hospital, but the doctor told her to go and look for someone who could pray because it was not a case of medication.

The question is, why did a believer who goes to church experience such a terrible nightmare and oppression? It was because there was a ladder in his life through which the enemy came in.

At this juncture, close your eyes and pray thus:

*Every satanic ladder hiding in my life, O God arise and let them be scattered, in the name of Jesus.*

If you have ever experienced being pressed down like this, lay your right hand on your head and pray like this,

*I fire back every arrow of oppression, in the name of Jesus.*

These powers know the background of your family, they know that only a few or none have made it, hence they say, "can any good thing come out of this life?"

Please, confess loudly: "I will make it, in Jesus' name." "I reject spiritual anaemia."

They do historical analysis of one's life and they know for

example, that nobody has ever built a house and you are trying to build one. They see that nobody has ever achieved a position of influence from that town or village of yours, and they perceive that this one wants to have a different record from others; then they say; "Can any good thing come out of this life?

Perhaps, the council of wickedness has spent sleepless nights to ensure that you do not move ahead. Then, you need to pray that your God should arise to scatter any evil council against you.

Perhaps, they have been conspiring against you and questioning your life. God is capable of changing your history, He can make His face to shine upon you.

The report of the Lord concerning us says, "They shall see ...", like Philip said, "Come and see", to the statement of Nathaniel who asked him saying, "Can any good thing come out of Nazareth?"

These are the days of high voltage praying, as Mr death is working an overtime, killing people before they attain their destiny, this Mr. death does not joke with people. He has been winning in the arena of human lives from the time of Adam till the present time, he has no respect for anybody.

There is a remedy for everything on earth, but there is no remedy for death, and one of the greatest tragedy is that so many people die for nothing. Another tragedy is that death uses our spoons and forks as his weapons. Unfortunately, death would accept no bribe from anybody. Like I said earlier, you have no right to die if you have not fulfilled your destiny.

This is not the time for myopic plans and weak vision, but the time to mount up with wings as eagle and if satan keeps reminding you about your problem, then you too should keep reminding him of his defeat.

For example, if Mr. Boyo wants to go to Togo, he can get there by road, air and sea - three ways. But somebody does not want Mr. Boyo to get to Togo, therefore, he plans many strategies to achieve this. Firstly, he incapacitates and demobilizes him with sickness and ignorance thereby rendering him unable to travel.

The bottom line is that Mr. Boyo should not get to Togo. In the alternative, he could outrightly kill Mr. Boyo since his objective is to cause him never to get to Togo. He may bewitch him such that Mr. Boyo is totally unconscious of any urge to go to Togo. He could physically hold him down or hinder him. He could attack all his vehicles and render them unworkable, the objective is still that Boyo must not get to Togo.

This serves to illustrate to us that the confidence of the

enemy rests solely on the fact that once they have destroyed one's vehicle of destiny, they know there is no way such a person can reach his goal because they have blocked all the avenues of getting there.

# EXAMPLES FROM THE SCRIPTURES

Let us look at a few Biblical examples.

*Rahab* - She was a harlot, but her vehicle of destiny were her hospitality. It was tied to hiding the spies from Israel and the rope with which she let down those spies to escape. Supposing she shunned those spies, that could have been the end of her destiny. We would not be reading today that she was part of the lineage of Jesus.

*King David* - David's vehicle of destiny was his divine curiosity, that is, his quest to know what was happening in the battlefield and who was Goliath to be harassing the people of God? He was left in the field to look after the sheep while his elderly brothers went to the war front. But, those senior brothers could not perform on the battlefield until he got there, and of course, the challenge of Goliath was the promotion of David.

Also, the hatred and pursuit of Saul after David was another vehicle of destiny for David. This means that the vehicle of your destiny may sometimes be very unfriendly, it may be things you do not enjoy or dislike in your life.

*Apostle Peter* - Peter's vehicle of destiny was his fishing job, he did it all the night, and it implied that he was not a lazy person. He was a generous person too. For, when Jesus asked him to release his boat to Him, he did not complain of not being able to catch any fish the previous night. Also, his boldness and humility to follow Jesus inspite of the fact that, at sixty six years old, his age doubled the age of Jesus Christ in the physical.

*Prophet Elisha* - Elisha's vehicle of destiny was his hard work, his loyalty to his master, his stubborn faith and his vigilance which made him to follow Elijah and get the double portion. What a glorious thing for him? And how shameful was it for Gehazi who could have got four times the anointing of Elijah. But instead, he collected leprosy, thus putting his posterity in trouble!

*Gideon* - Gideon, another man of destiny, was working hard in the midst of the enemy, when the angel came unto him and said, ". . . peace unto you great man of valour . . .." He was not cajoled by the angel's statement. He said, "Which peace? when, what I am doing here is in the secret of our oppressors . . .." His openness and admission of helplessness was his vehicle of destiny. His readiness to carry out divine instruction to the letter was his vehicle of destiny too.

*Mary Magdalene* - What was Mary Magdalene's vehicle of destiny? Her demons of course. From her, Jesus cast out seven demons. So, satan made one of the greatest mistakes of his life when he invaded Mary Magdalene. Some people complain: "If you know the kind of deliverance I have done in the past . . ." Well, if such people properly examine it, they would discover that such deliverance may turn out to be their vehicles of destiny. It was the deliverance of this woman that made her to be the first person to see the Lord Jesus when He rose from the dead. Her seeking for deliverance became the vehicle of her destiny.

*Joseph* - Joseph's vehicle of destiny was envy and jealousy of his brothers. Even his father cautioned him to desist from talking about his dream. He queried, "how can I and your mother be bowing down for you?" False accusation was also his vehicle of destiny. Later on, when he got to prison, he told Pharaoh's butler that he was going to be released and that he should remember him. But the Bible says the man forgot Joseph in the prison after his release. We understand here that broken promises also added to his vehicles of destiny.

Say this loud and clear: *"My problem is my promotion."*

# HOW TO DELIVER VEHICLES OF DESTINY

How can we become an overcomer against forces of demotion? How can we deliver our vehicles of destiny? Because you need a vehicle to convey you from where you are to your place of destiny. For, if the enemy destroys that vehicle, the person will become grounded.

## *THROUGH DREAMS*

We look at this in many ways, by examining our dreams and destiny. In Psalm 32:8,

> I will instruct thee and teach thee in the way which thou shalt go: I will guide thee with mine eye.

It is unfortunate to discover that very few people receive instruction from the Lord. Some come to the church to pick the ones they like in the words of God and leave others, some do not even listen to anything at all. Others are only interested in selling their wares in the church than to pray against the spirit of poverty hunting their lives. The passage tells us that we should not move if we do not receive an instruction from the Lord to do so.

If verse eight of this chapter is not in operation in one's life, then verse nine goes into operation in the reverse thus,

> Be ye not as the horse, or as the mule, which have no

understanding: whose mouth must be held in with bit and bridle, lest they come near unto thee.

That is telling us that some people have no understanding. This is also in Job 33:13-14:

Why dost thou strive against him? for he giveth not account of any of his matters. For God speaketh once, yea twice, yet man perceiveth it not.

That is, God talks to us and we do not get His message most of the time, because there are so many different levels of communication as shown in verses 15-16:

In a dream, in a vision of the night, when deep sleep falleth upon men, in slumberings upon the bed; Then he openeth the ears of men, and sealeth their instruction,

In the light of the above passage, your dreams can tell you a lot of things, it can be a source of divine instruction to you for your destiny. That is why the Bible confirms that the almighty would do nothing except He first reveals it to his prophets. This is stated in Amos 3:7:

Surely the Lord GOD will do nothing, but he revealeth his secret unto his servants the prophets.

It is one thing for God to pass an information like this to his servants, it is another thing whether you understand it or not. God desires to talk to His people, but when He discovers we do not understand him through some medium of communication, He then resorts to seal His instruction to us through dreams.

Say this loud and pray like this,

*As many enemies as lay their rods on the altar, my rod shall swallow them.*

*In every battle that I fight, I shall be more than conquerors.*

Through your dreams, you can know whether your vehicle of destiny is under attack. By the time a person is sixty years old, he would have spent twenty years sleeping. You spend one third of your life's span sleeping.

What happened during this sleeping period should not be taken lightly. Because, those dreams that occurred then are visions and they reveal our deepest aims and objectives. It is like a kind of spiritual monitoring system which aids you to deal with your physical life.

Those dreams can also reveal your fears, aspirations, hopes, past life and your future. It can result in your healing, it can change and influence your life. Those dreams can enlighten, warn and inform you. Therefore, they should not be ignored, the only dreams that you could ignore are dreams you had after you had been agitated the previous day.

For example, if you had conjugal quarrel before you went

to sleep, you can ignore any dream you have that night.

The dreams you have as a result of swallowing chloroquine for malaria fever or after overeating or when you sleep in an occultic and demonic apartment, should be ignored in their entirety.

Apart from all these, all other dreams are divine tools through which divine messages are brought to you. It may be from you, God or the devil.

A well-read Bible scholar would discover that there are twenty-eight accounts of dreams in the Bible. The first example of dreaming is an interesting thing. Somebody wanted to take over Abraham's wife and the Lord came to the man in the dream, saying, "Abimelech, you are a dead man" He asked the Lord what he had done, then the Lord told him because the woman he took into his house was another man's wife.

The Lord said, "It is because I like you, that is why I have restrained you from committing sin with her. The Lord told him to return the wife adding, "I have told the husband to pray for you for he is a prophet". This marked the first time to find the words, "Pray for someone," in the Bible.

Jacob was a confused man until he had a dream wherein he saw a ladder upon which angels of God were descending and ascending and he remarked, ". . . surely, the Lord is in this place."

Joseph was nicknamed, 'the dreamer' in the Bible. It was his dreams that put him into trouble. Also, it was the angel of God who told Joseph the earthly father of Jesus to take the child and flee with him to Egypt.

This reminds me of a question once asked by a sister. She asked is she should continue to visit her people who are mostly witches and wizards in her village. Or should she still run away from them? God who could command Herod to be roasted did not do it but instead told Joseph to carry his baby and run. This is telling us that there is time for running and there is time for fighting.

The Bible even says further that God can use your dreams to torment your enemy, and that was what happened to Pilate's wife. She told her husband about how she suffered in the dream because of that righteous man, Jesus.

Paul, in the midst of tempest and threat of ship-wreckage told the people concerning the dream he had in the night that the angel of God appeared unto him to allay his fear that no life would be lost in the voyage. Right from that moment, Paul had supernatural confidence.

We need revelation knowledge to overcome our

problems. To be informed is to be transformed. You may claim, you have no problem but it can mean three things - the world has given you a 'red card', that is, you have been asked to depart from the 'field of play' or God has forgotten you or satan too has rejected you. All the people of God in the Bible faced certain things and overcame them. Even the Bible says, "Let God arise and let all His enemies scatter."

How then can you claim you do not have problems? The truth is, any man without an enemy is a nonentity, zombie and an unimaginable idiot. It shows you are not useful to anybody. Immediately you make an attempt to mount up with wings as eagle, there will be forces that are ready to counter your move. However, an interesting thing in the Bible is that every Pharaoh has his own Moses, every Goliath has his own David and every head of Goliath has an unprotected forehead.

# DREAMS THAT INDICATE DESTINIES THAT ARE UNDER ATTACK

There are twelve major dreams that indicate that your vehicle of destiny is under an attack. Let me share these with you so that you can know how to pray.

*Lack of dreams*. That is very dangerous because in the face of danger and troubles, you do not have information. It means the enemy has blinded your spirit man and soul. Such people die like houseflies for being ignorant of what transpires in their spirit system. I prayed with a sister sometime ago and when she got home, she dreamt of seeing herself in the palace of a king and the evil king said "By going to that man (referring to me) for prayer, does it mean that the church you are attending now is not good?"

He then told her, "If you go there again, you will no longer dream." This sister thought it was a joke, but afterwards, there was no dreaming in her life again. That evil spirit knew that the best way you can quickly eliminate a person is to withdraw dreaming from his or her life.

Somebody who dreamt of being pursued would wake up to start fighting back. The one who dreamt seeing his child being thrown into the river would soon wake up to reverse it. But if you do not see anything, they will just begin to operate unchallenged for lack of information on your part.

Sometimes, I took a flight wherein the pilot just took off recklessly in the sky. However, as far as I am concerned, I had already checked up my own monitoring system, I got it clear that I was not going to die in an aircraft. As the plane was diving up and down in the sky, I was confident that there was not going to be any mishap, and so, I was reading my book when someone tapped me and said,

". . . Mr. Man, what book are you reading in this situation?"

Then I said,

"Sir, this plane will not crash, because I have checked up my monitoring system; if it crashes, you will end up being the only casualty, so don't disturb me, let me read my book."

When the plane eventually landed, he came to me and asked,

"Are you a human being?"

You become a weaponless warrior when your dreams are wiped off.

***Dreams that cannot be recalled.*** That is, some people can no longer remember what they dreamt about when they wake up. Their memory system is either faulty or damaged. They know that they had a dream, but cannot recall it. This is another terrible thing.

Close your eyes and pray like this,

***My dream life, receive the fire of God, in the name of Jesus.***

[123]

There are situations when an incident occurs and someone would say, "Ah, I saw this thing before." Because he could not remember, he could not stand against it to prevent it from happening.

***Dreams of retreating back to childhood days***. These are the powers of retardation. They are the powers responsible for making a person not to exceed a particular stage in life. When you keep seeing either your nursery and primary schools or the old house your family lived when you were a small girl or boy, something is telling you that you are not moving. You need to wage a war because you are being told that your vehicle of destiny is under attack.

***Rags wearing or nakedness***. This is the spirit of poverty, embarrassment and shame. When a man goes to school and struggles to study to become a lawyer, but at the end of the day, all he could afford is a second-hand piece of suit coupled with cheap perfumes they sell at the bus stops, he should know that his vehicle of destiny is under attack. How about doctors without clinics and when they manage to have one, they employ demonic nurses who drink the blood of patients, thus rendering the place desolate.

A person who is supposed to be operating a supermarket is hawking pure water by the road side. These are the examples of what we are talking about. But if they can check up, God would have shown them in His mercy, only they cannot recognize that God has been talking to them.

*Being caged, imprisoned or hindered*. These are forces of limitation. They put the person in a pit without water. These are dreams of retrogression and of being confined by the enemy. This is a popular weapon in our environment that we must wage war against.

*Always dreaming of serving others*. In other words, it is the spirit of slavery, the person will always be a servant to others. Many of us do not like the situation we are in, but we are not desperate and mad with it yet in prayer.

*Dreams of uncompleted task*. In the case of an examination he could not finish until they stopped. When building a house it is uncompleted and when travelling he does not know his direction. This is a vagabond anointing. It is a terrible dream showing that the vehicle of destiny of that person is under terrible attack.

*Having sex in the dreams*. These are dreams connected with marital turbulence and the destiny of such victim is being manipulated. It also implies that God's power is being withdrawn from such life. It also means either partner's potential has been buried.

A man once fasted and prayed for seven days but ended with fornication on the final day. As he was breaking his seven days dry fast, a child of the devil walked in and he capped the programme with fornication! During interrogation, we found out he had been having sexual dreams before. It is when some people have an important business to transact that they begin to have sex in their dreams, such business will surely collapse.

*Death in the dream*. This means that the enemy has closed the chapter of such life. It could result in spiritual, physical, financial, and marital death - all departments in his life have been shut down. Seeing dead relatives in dreams is an indication that you have very strong ancestral spirits link which you should break.

*Seeing tortoise or snail regularly in the dream*. It means slow progress, procrastination and all good things are suffering postponement. It is tortoise and snail anointing.

*Being pursued by animals or masquerade*. This is witchcraft attack.

*Dreaming of water*. It shows that the fellow has linkage with marine spirits.

If you have been having these kinds of dreams, it shows your vehicle of destiny is under attack. It means some powers somewhere or some human agents have decided that such a person cannot move.

These powers are often successful because many

Christians are not serious. They are playing with sins. Anyone who goes to a Bible believing church where they preach holiness and transformation of lives, whose life is not changed, then his destiny would not change too until he repents and becomes an example of holiness. Everybody needs to repent of giving the enemy a foothold to operate. Then, renounce every conscious and unconscious contact with destiny destroyers. Wage war against them.

Let me warn that if a person is living in a known sin and you want to attack destiny destroyer, you will only end up strengthening them except you repent.

# PRAYER POINTS

1. Every power threatening my destiny, be broken, in the name of Jesus.

2. My destiny, escape from every prison, in the name of Jesus.

3. O God arise, let every witchcraft plantation scatter, in the name of Jesus.

## Your Foundation and Your Destiny

We are all familiar with the rest of the story. Pharaoh's sorcerers and magicians were all soundly disgraced.

The Old Testament saints who lived under an inferior covenant acted like gods even though Christ was yet to come, His blood had not been shed and the Holy Spirit had not descended. When God told Moses that He had made him a god unto Pharaoh, Moses acted just like a god.

This fact leaps at us when we read in the Bible of how Joshua stopped the sun and also about a man called Elijah who locked up the rain for three and a half years and put the key in his pocket, saying, "There shall be no rain nor dew on this land except by my words." For this, King Ahab sent for him so that he could be persuaded to re-open the heavens.

These men acted like mini-gods and caused things to happen. Sometimes, it would appear that they even created problems for God as they decreed one thing and God hastened to bring it to pass.

There used to be a powerful warrior called Napoleon. He conquered many places, and when there were no more places to conquer he started crying. It was Napoleon who grabbed the world map, pointed to China and said, "There lies a sleeping giant; let it sleep, because if it should wake up, it would shake the world." That prophecy made by

Napoleon two **hund**red years ago, when viewed critically now, makes sense. If we look at the population of China, whenever it rises up, it should overpower the rest of the world.

## THE FEAR OF THE ENEMY

Today, beloved, Lucifer is busy surveying our world, just like Napoleon surveyed China. And you can see the fear in the eye of the enemy as he realises the potentials of the power you will wield if you should ever wake up.

I wonder what would have happened in Nigeria if we had about four Elijahs: one in the North, one in the South, one in the East and one in the West so that when we wish to fight all he would do is call fire to fall down, and everybody would disperse. But where is such power?

The enemy is looking at us with fear, and wondering when we God's chosen people, would ever wake up, because he knows that the moment we wake up, he will be in serious trouble.

For instance, if you have prayed for the Holy Ghost baptism for three years without receiving it, it means something somewhere is afraid of you.

drunk, neither did he commit murder, nor ,eal. **His** problem was that he simply fell asleep. And the sleep was so deep that when the 'barbers' were working on him he never woke up. In fact, he did not wake up until they had completely scraped everything on his head. The only time he woke up was when his wife Delilah, the fire extinguisher, shouted,

"The Philistines come unto this house!"

Then he said,

"I will arise, at other times."

And the Bible says, "He did not know that the Spirit of God had deserted him."

The Spirit of God left Samson after the witchcraft barbers had worked on his head. But, indeed, his problem started when he fell asleep. Of course, if he had remained awake, he would not have allowed them to touch his head.

That singular act of Samson scattered the forces of the true and living God. God must have been so disappointed; likewise his parents who had the prophecy of angels before giving birth to him.

It is sad but it is true that this is the most prayerless generation since the Pentecost. This is because it is one age when Christians are more comfortable than they used to

**be**. Our problem is still the problem of the garden of Gethesemane! Sleep, spiritual slumber. And our cry these days should be: Where is the God of Elijah? Let Him manifest His power!

In front of one of our new churches in the east is an evil tree where 75% of the community gather to worship the idol in the tree. Standing at the MFM church, one can easily see the tree. So, after service each day, the man of God there would say, "Please, pray this prayer, f. o. c. (free of charge): 'Every evil tree, growing for my sake, dry up, in Jesus' name.

One day, however, they noticed that smoke was coming out from the root of that evil tree. Quickly, they went to call the chief priest. He took buckets of water and started quenching the fire burning under the tree. But the more he poured water, the more the fire grew. Then, as if God was trying to show him that water was not the problem, rain now started to fall seriously, yet, the fire kept burning.

The fire raged for about ten days and the tree was completely destroyed. The people got annoyed and went to the main oracle to ask it where it was when its younger brother was burning.

Then the oracle said that the people who burnt that tree were the new church near it; so the people needed to be

those who sleep during church service. My report showed that the first group of people who sleep in the church are those who eat in their dream. This makes them easily sleep off.

Then the second group are those who watch television till midnight only to come to church to catch up on their sleep.

The third group are those who take drugs.

The fourth group is made up of those who simply lack interest in what goes on in the church. However, should you announce that the topic of the sermon for the day is 'how to convert Naira into Dollars; these people are not likely to fall asleep. But for as long as the topic remains how to make heaven, they are sure to fall asleep.

The fifth group are those who work the night shift. This category of people should pray go God to give them the kind of work that will enable them serve Him.

Then, we have the other group of people who have received satanic arrows which would make it difficult for them to gain anything from any church service. This is made possible when they keep sleeping when the angels arrive.

Another group are those who are already deep in spiritual slumber.

# HOW TO OPERATE LIKE GOD

How do we operate and exercise the power that God has given us? The first key is discipline.

## ➥ DISCIPLINE - The Operational Word

You are not likely to make any progress until you learn to discipline yourself.

When Apostle Paul started his ministry, he started with a three-day fast. Just how many Christians have done this when they got born again?

Those of us who have read about the great Apostle Babalola must have read about how he went into a three-day fast when he was called by God. As he was about to break, God told him to go into a nineteen-day fast.

Without discipline we cannot become what God wants us to be. You need to discipline so many aspects of your life: your emotions, temper, dressing and reading of the Bible. The haphazard reading of the Bible must stop;

So what we need now is discipline. The Apostle Paul was a disciplinarian like his Master.

*He disciplined his body.* Likewise, if you desire to be like little gods on earth you have to discipline your body. Of course, the body would want to do what it wants to do

[139]

see signs and wonders."

When we say "supernatural", we mean something that works against nature itself, a law higher than nature itself.

### ➡ WATCH YOUR WORDS

We need to watch our words. Words are the most powerful things in creation. The way we use our words will dictate whether we will operate as gods or as men.

That is why powerful prophets of God are generally not talkative. If you come across a person who calls himself a man of God and he is talkative, his closeness to God should be doubted seriously. God Himself is not talkative. He says what He means and means what He says, and He has no time for any form of argument.

Words are very powerful.

When I was a small boy, I saw something at a popular bus stop in Lagos in the early 70s. There was a mad cow on rampage and everyone ran helter-skelter to avoid an attack from it.

All of a sudden, a bus conductor who had been calling passengers into his bus, jumped down and walked straight to this mad cow and started to talk to it. As he spoke to that cow it was as if someone poured cold water on the animal, because the cow calmly sat down in the middle of the street. A child of the devil spoke words to a mad cow and sat it down. The bus conductor had that power yet he was a poor man. How about the children of God?

Words are so powerful that the Bible says, "In the beginning, was the word, and the word was with God." And as that word is said, it decides for us whether we will live in victory or live as the vanquished.

Many of us use our mouth to defeat ourselves day by day. After serious prayer sessions, many cancel their prayers by their words. After serious prayers, many say they get annoyed, jump down from their car and begin to shout at other drivers.

Many have prayed defeat and failure and have received both. How is this possible? Of course, when a man begins to pray, saying, "O Lord, what have I done to You that my own life is so hard? O God, if You know that You will not answer my prayer, why not kill me?"

These, obviously are the devil's prayer points and all the person can get from the devil is encouragement to carry on with such prayers. So when a man keeps praying defeat and failure, you are only advertising the devil's power. Whereas if you control your tongue and bring it under the subjection of the Holy Ghost, you will become like God.

How did God create the heaven and the earth? He spoke

[143]

words, "Let there be..." and there was. When God says, "Let there be...", it means the thing was not there before; He brings the visible out of the invisible. When He says, "Come out of or come forth...," it means that thing must manifest as He has commanded.

Throughout the Bible, God never did anything without saying them.

The enemy knows immediately you realise the power in your words and begin to use it, he is in trouble completely. This is why he tries to speak the words of defeat and fear into people's lives because he knows that there is nothing so powerful or so great that words cannot control.

I once shared the testimony of a sister who was kidnaped. When she began to pray, her captors warned her to stop. She had seen these people kill others in her presence and how they cut their breast and gogged out their eyes. Though she kept quiet, her lips still moved.

For the third time, they came to warn her to keep quiet. Now the sister kept quiet and started praying in her heart. Yet, the kidnappers came back to ask why she kept doing the same thing they warned her not to do.

Eventually, the power of God visited the place, scattered what they were doing like a whirlwind. This paved way for the sister to run out. She was kidnaped from Lagos, but she found herself at Ore (some three hundred kilometers away).

The circumstances surrounding every human being can be controlled by the words of God concealed in the laboratory of the heart and spoken out in faith.

Satan is a fallen angel who has no creative power. He seeks to use the power delegated to man and manipulate it to his own advantage. Only God knows how many cases believers have used their mouths to destroy. Your words are the vehicles of your future.

When a person is carrying out a project and he is asked how it is going, if he says, "Not too bad," it means it is already bad. Negative words like these create problems, and we need to do something about them. You must change your words to align with what God wants.

## HOW DO YOU GET YOUR CREATIVE POWER INTO OPERATION?

*Study and search the Bible for promises that pertain to you as a believer*. Do not be the kind of Christian who has the Psalms in his Bible dirty while the other areas are clean.

Make a list of these promises. This may not be sound as easy as it sounds because the devil will bring a big battle into your life. Compile the promises and read them like a daily ritual. When you read them loud and hear them with your ears, something happens to your spirit. Confidence comes into your spirit and builds something there. As you keep reading them, they become established in your life and become part of you.

Many people are able to remember a lot of things, but when it comes to the Bible they easily forget. This is due to the activity of the devil that does not want the Holy Spirit to be established in their lives.

For instance, when an impromptu test is conducted for a lot of people to name the twelve disciples, many are bound to fail. But when the question comes to naming the members of the national football team, many will not only name all those on the playing field, but will also readily say the names of those on the reserved bench.

So, the enemy does not want anybody to eat or swallow the Scriptures because he knows that the more you swallow it, the more you get powerful in the spirit. It takes time and efforts for Bible reading to become natural for anyone. But as it builds in your spirit things begin to happen for you.

So, what secret am I sharing here? It is that as you continually say what God is saying, as you continually soak your spirit in what God is saying, you begin to change. It may take you days, weeks, months or years, depending on how badly you had programmed your spirit before, but immediately you begin to speak faithful words, it will begin to do great things for you.

Many of us need to re-arrange our vocabulary and programme our language. Jesus spoke and things began to happen. Any Christian who operates perpetually at the level of the flesh will never become a mini-god.

"Is it not written in your law, I say unto you, Ye are gods?"

A brother got into his bedroom and found that everything had been scattered. As he was wondering why it was scattered, he saw the devil standing in one corner. This angered him and he said,

"Mr. devil, when I left this place in the morning, my bed was in this corner, my chair was in that corner; why did you change the positions of things behind me? Right now, I want you to put things back in their rightful positions!"

As he spoke, things began to happen. The devil re-arranged what he had scattered.

The enemy is afraid that if these people understand what they are, they will shake strongholds. Who is a witch when the power of God is upon your life? How can a hen decide to go and lay eggs in a place where there is fire? How can you plug your pressing iron into electricity till it gets hot, only for a mosquito to come and land on its hot surface?

When you become too hot to handle they are bound to leave you alone. The reason they are still harassing you is that they can handle you, but when you become too hot to handle, they will leave you alone.

At this point, let me ask you one question: Do you want to live this kind of mountain-top life? Or you want to keep struggling in the valley? What is your answer?

## PRAYER POINTS

1. O thou that troubleth my Isreal, my God shall trouble you today, in the name of Jesus.

2. Every serpent despatched against my destiny, die! in the name of Jesus.

3. Every bird of darkness picking the word of God from my heart, I shoot you down, in the name of Jesus.

4. (Lay your right hand on your head) Power of God,

incubate my life, in the name of Jesus.

5. Every power draining my spiritual blood, what are you waiting for? Die, in the name of Jesus.

6. I claim a turn-around breakthrough by fire, in the name of Jesus.

# YOUR DREAMS AND
# YOUR DESTINY

## Your Foundation and Your Destiny

But while men slept, his enemy came and sowed tares among the wheat, and went his way (Matthew 13:25).

*We* can see from the above verse that the visit paid to man while he slept was far from being a friendly one. It was a visit paid to plant something in his life; and the enemy had chosen a particular time to do this: while men slept. This means that some of the greatest dangers that we face as human beings happen during sleep.

Why dost thou strive against him? for he giveth not account of any of his matters. [14]For God speaketh once, yea twice, yet man perceiveth it not. [15]In a dream, in a vision of the night, when deep sleep falleth upon men, in slumberings upon the bed; [16]Then he openeth the ears of men, and sealeth their instruction, [17]That he may withdraw man from his purpose, and hide pride from man. [18]He keepeth back his soul from the pit, and his life from perishing by the sword (Job 33:13-18).

What the above passage has been telling us is that while God talks to us at many times many of us do not perceive what He is saying, technically because our lives are too noisy, and because this does not allow us to hear Him when we should, He now goes into our dream to talk to us so that, if there is any bad thing we desire to do, he may restrain us from going ahead.

Two words stand out in the above passage: destiny and dream. What is your destiny? Your destiny is the reason why you were born. What is you destiny? Your destiny is the purpose of God for your life. Destiny can also be defined as what God has written in his book concerning your life. Jesus said, "the son of man goeth as is written of him," meaning that your destiny is when you go as it is written of you. Which means, also, that it is possible to go as it is not written.

# WHAT IS YOUR DESTINY?

Your destiny is what God had in mind before He created you and asked you to come into this world.

It is God's pre-ordained plan for your life. One way or the other, your destiny is already programmed by the Almighty. But then, it can be diverted, destroyed, perverted, smashed to pieces or fragmented. That is part of the reasons you must read this with absolute concentration.

The second part of the passage quoted above talks about dreams:

. . .while men slept his enemy came and sowed tares . . .

I pray that every implantation by the enemy shall be uprooted from your life, in the name of Jesus.

Most sleeping takes place at night, and the most dangerous period of the night is between 2a.m and 3a.m. Fortunately and unfortunately, however, that is the hour that most people sleep deeply.

## WHY OPERATION AT NIGHT

The enemy chooses the night because the night is characterized by darkness.

The night is also characterized by intense spiritual activities. Workers in the dark kingdom are desperate at that hour to fulfil their quota.

The midnight is the time when most human beings are least alert.

The night, therefore, is a very favourable period for the plans of the wicked; and the Lord knows this, and the enemy knows this as well.

## SALIENT POINTS

I wish to make some statements about dreams so that we can know for sure where we are going and know how to pray.

Your dreams can determine your destiny. God, in His own infinite mercies, designed for man to have dreams. Therefore, if you look at your Bible, you will find dreams mentioned 121 times.

By the time a person is sixty years old he will have spent

twenty years sleeping. And since one-third of our lifetime is spent sleeping, it means that a large percentage of our life is spent dreaming as dreaming occurs during sleep.

➡ Dreams are important in human life.

➡ Dreams are visions during sleep.

➡ Dreams are revelation of some little portions of the activities of the spirit world.

➡ Dreams are scenes of occurrences in the spirit realm. The image we see in the dream are transactions that go on during sleep.

➡ Your dream puts you in touch with some internal security system, with your internal wisdom.

➡ Your dream will open your spiritual life to you. And these dreams do not lie.

➡ Dreams are the windows to your unconscious feelings and to your unconscious thoughts. Many of us do not know what is happening in our lives because we don't understand our dreams.

➡ Dreams should reveal our deepest aims and objectives.

➡ It is a spiritual monitoring system which helps you to deal with your physical life.

## Your Foundation and Your Destiny

➡ Your dreams should reveal to you your fears and your hopes.

➡ It should reveal your past to you and your future.

➡ Your dream can heal you, change you and influence your life.

➡ Your dream can enlighten you; it can warn you or inform you.

Because of all these, dreams are important and should not be ignored. Any dream you have consistently should be taken serious.

These dreams are the invisible tools that bring messages to you. It is your spiritual monitoring system, by which you can know what is happening to your life in the spiritual world.

A brother found it difficult to pass his examinations, so he started praying. Any time he dreamt, he would always see this goat tied to a tree. He never understood this.

He got born again, went to Bible school for ten years where they preached holiness, faith and what have you. Yet, he kept seeing this goat tied to a tree and as much as the goat struggled to get free, the rope held it back. Yet, this brother did not understand until one day when he came to a prayer meeting where somebody preached this kind of message.

He then understood that the goat he was seeing was him, and the rope that tied it to the tree was the enemy's boundary for his life. He could not go beyond that rope nor move far; he had been caged.

Then the brother started praying hard. All of a sudden, his uncle visited from the village and asked to talk to the brother. The uncle asked him whether he recently went to see a herbalist. The brother said no. The uncle couldn't believe this so he asked further,

"Has anyone recently told you anything about your life?"

The brother, again, said no.

Then the uncle asked,

"Then, what happened to the goat?"

The brother asked what his uncle meant by the goat but the man brushed the matter aside. But the brother would not let the matter pass just like that. Putting holiness aside for a while, the brother held on to his uncle's shirt and, shaking him violently, asked him to expatiate on the goat which he just mentioned.

It happened that the day the brother was born this uncle of his was at home. Through his demonic power he could see into the future of that brother. He therefore programmed his life into a goat and put the goat at the backyard. Whenever a goat died he tied another one down and re-programmed it.

All of a sudden, however, the goat made a strange cry and died where it was tied. It was then this brother began to move ahead. All along, his dream had been telling him that his destiny was in bondage but he did not understand. Then, he remembered the word of the prophet, "My people perish for lack of knowledge."

In your dreams is where you work out your pains, griefs, and hostilities. When something is being hostile to you, you can see. The land of slumber, therefore, is as important as life itself.

# SCRIPTURAL ACCOUNTS

There are, at least, twenty-eight accounts in the Bible, in the Old Testament, about dreams.

The first example in the Bible is Genesis 20. In Genesis 28 where Jacob saw the ladder.

Then there was the dream of Joseph. The destiny of Joseph was made clear to him in his dream, but the only problem was that the boy refused to keep quiet. He kept talking.

Pharaoh also dreamt about famine in Egypt but he could not interpret it.

Solomon, too, dreamt and God asked him to chose wisdom which he wanted.

Those wise men that came to Jesus saw certain things in their dream.

Paul, on his missionary journey, saw a man beckoning at him, inviting him to come to Macedonia to help them.

Pilate's wife had a dream that tormented her. She went to tell the husband not to touch Jesus Christ.

Ninety-nine percent of the Revelation knowledge that we need in order to overcome our problems can be revealed to us in the dream; and it is said that to be informed is to be transformed.

Dreams can come from God. It can come from man. It can also come from the enemy.

When the dream is from God, the dreamer is left normal, calm, quiet, reasonable, with open and clear mind after that dream. And if it is the Almighty talking to you in the dream, He will give you:

➡ assurance;

➡ encourage you;

➡ comfort you;

➡ give you directions;

➡ instruct you;

➡ guide you;

➡ exhort you;

➡ correct you;

➡ show you the future;

➡ reveals His plans and purposes to you.

If it is from your enemy or satan, the dream will be mysterious, absurd, sometimes empty, sometime foolish, sometimes leaving the person confused and dazed. the dream would be so unreasonable, most time it would not make any sense; sometimes it is so mysterious that you wonder what kind of dream it is .

It is like that sister who had a dream that she was sitting on a mat while another woman sat on another mat. Both of them were flying. She was asking the woman at the front section of the mat,

"Why am I on this mat and where am I going?

The woman said,

"When you get there, you will know. But it's not good for one to be flying on a mat."

The woman did not answer her anymore. So the sister began to pray. At one point, it was as if a rope cut in that mat, and the sister landed on the ground. Then she woke up with pains in her back. What was going to happen to her? They were taking her to a witchcraft meeting to initiate her unconsciously.

When your dream is an attack from the enemy, it can represent satanic strategy to cause calamity and destruction.

And when you have dream attack from the enemy, the enemy attacks for seven reasons.

➡ to steal, kill and to destroy;

➡ to terrify;

➡ to inflict terrible sicknesses.

A lot of people wake from an attack in the dream and the sickness takes root immediately.

➡ to contact a covenant from the devil;

➡ to deceive men.

The Bible says, 'marvel not' because satan himself can present himself as an angel of light;

➡ to cause man to take the wrong decision;

➡ to terminate destinies.

Beloved, it is a serious matter when God is showing you the pictures of your life and you don't know what to do. Fortunately, there is a way out because in the spiritual world where you find fast forward and rewind functions. This is not like a physical house.

For instance, as you sit down in a place, you cannot decide to be ten years younger. This is not possible. But in the spirit world, you can do a rewind to when you were ten years old. Likewise, you can do a fast forward to see what will happen in ten years' time.

A sister was praying to marry. she was already 39years old, yet no man had ever proposed to her. So she continued praying. Then God took her back to when she was fifteen years old, at a particular birthday party. She was serving the guests the birthday cake. When she got to a man, the man took the first, second, third cake. This made the sister protest. But instead of the man dropping the excess pieces of cake, he drew the girl close and told her.

"You're my wife. If you don't marry me, you won't marry anybody."

That incident happened when she was fifteen years old but she did not know the importance of it until she started praying at the age of 39 when the Lord took her back 24 years.

## DANGER OF NOT DREAMING

If you don't dream at all, or you feel you don't dream at all, there is double danger:

➤ If God wants to talk to you, you will not hear;

The enemy's presence and activities in your life will be hidden. Of course, it is that which you know that you would want to pray against. But as long as you don't know, you are in trouble. It is most dangerous in the day of danger and trouble for you not to have information at all.

The enemy has blinded the spirit man and soul of so many people that when they wake up they forget everything they dreamt of. In fact, scientists agree that everybody dreams. The only problem is that you may have the inability to recall your dreams.

Paul was on the sea, and it seemed as if all hopes were lost. But he had a dream. In the dream, an angel of the Lord stood by him, telling him not to fear as nobody would die inside that ship. Immediately Paul had that dream, he rose up an asked people to eat and drink as no one on the ship would die.

If you don't have signs like this as a Christian, you become a weaponless warrior. The enemy has tampered with your spiritual monitoring system. If you suffer from the inability to recall dreams, it is a serious problem that you must pray over.

Right at this moment, a particular power is afraid of you and doesn't want you to have certain information, you will act like fire and thunder. And because they don't want you to act, the best thing, they feel, is to make you forget. This is a very serious matter.

If many of us could know what is going on in our dream life we will understand what is going on in our physical life.

# DREAMS TO IGNORE

Nevertheless, there are some dreams that you can ignore.

For example,

➥ Any dream you had in a night you were very agitated should be forgotten.

➥ Any dream that you have when you have malaria should likewise not be taken seriously.

➥ Any dream you have when you have over-feed yourself also qualifies for neglect.

➥ And when you dream while you sleep in an occultic house, simply forget that dream.

➥ Any dream you have after a family quarrel cannot be taken seriously.

➥ Any dream out of the multitude of business should be forgotten.

There is also something called dream within a dream. This happen when people have three or four dreams at a time that everything looks jumbled out that they can't make out the details of each one.

# EVIL AND BAD DREAMS

➤ If you dream and you find yourself drinking dirty water, it means the enemy wants to poison your spiritual life and reduce your fire.

➤ If you dream and see yourself drowning and crying for help, the enemy is planning tribulations for you.

➤ If you dream that something keeps obstructing you as you seek to cross from one place to another, the enemy is trying to hinder your progress.

➤ If you are always eating meat, the bottom line is that you have become a witch participating in witchcraft feeding.

And when you find yourself always eating, and your mouth is even forced open to take food in the dream, it means the enemy wants to weaken your spiritual power and plant sickness into your life.

Some years back we prayed for a sister who dreamt that she was breast-feeding a strange baby who held her breast with its teeth. She tried to push the baby away but the baby held tight to the breast. She then hit the baby on the head. As the baby dropped to the floor the sister woke up with pains. Before that week ran out, five lumps developed in that breast.

Unfortunately, before one week, the sister died. This was due largely to the fact that despite getting spiritual assistance from some men of God the sister still went about seeking solution in dark places.

➡ If you find yourself climbing a mountain with difficulty, it means the enemy is making you toil before you can survive.

➡ If you find yourself in a traffic hold-up, the enemy is introducing sluggishness into your life.

➡ And if you find yourself nursing a strange baby, or milking a strange baby, the enemy is drinking the milk of your life.

➡ If you find yourself falling into a pit and are unable to come out, the enemy has imprisoned you.

➡ If you find wind and whirlwind fighting against you, God is trying to tell you that there are troubles ahead to retard your progress.

➡ If you find that your cap was blown away by wind, it means disgrace is on its way for you.

➡ Or if you lose something very important like your shoes or sandals, marital disturbance is coming. You'd better start praying.

➡ If you find your documents stolen in the dream, the enemy is trying to make those documents useless.

➡ If you find that your clothes were stolen in the dream, this is an attack on your honour and glory.

➡ If you see yourself, in the dream, carrying a heavy load, the enemy is trying to introduce paralysing problems into your life, the kind of things that will make the person unable to move.

➡ If you find yourself always sitting for examinations but without finishing the examinations, this is the spirit of frustration and failure.

➡ If you find yourself in darkness in the dream, this represents spiritual blindness.

➡ If, in the dream, you find yourself being beaten by rain and you running from it, it means the enemy is trying to prepare trouble for you.

➡ When you dream and see fire destroying things, the enemy is trying to introduce calamity and woe into your life, you have to stop this.

➡ If you find that you are travelling and the road is becoming longer and longer and longer, and you never really finish that journey until you wake up, the enemy is only trying to introduce frustration into your life.

➡ If you find yourself being shot, either with arrow or gun, the enemy is trying to introduce afflictions of a terrible kind into your life.

➡ If you dream of wearing a rag, nobody needs to tell you that this is the spirit of poverty and lack.

➡ If you find yourself in an environment with faeces and dirty things around you, the enemy is trying to make you to miss heaven.

➡ If you find yourself naked in the dream, this is the coming of disgrace and insecurity.

➡ If you find your wedding ring and wedding gown stolen or torn or something bad happens to them, this is an attack on your marriage.

This is one reason why, at the Mountain of Fire and Miracles Ministries, we don't wed people with ring but the Bible because the wedding ring is a covenant material, and if the enemy can lay his hand on it, this can be used to easily detablise your home.

➡ If you find your keys stolen, this means, your enemy is trying to steal your spiritual authority from you.

➥ If you find your house being burgled and your things being stolen, the enemy is trying to introduce spiritual emptiness into your life.

➥ If you dream that a child is missing, you have to pray hard for that child not to die.

➥ If you dream and find a woman shaving your hair, you need to pray for the enemy not to kill your husband.

➥ If you keep dreaming of masquerades, that is witchcraft and ancestral spirits pursuing you.

➥ If you find that you are being attacked by dogs, these are sexual demons.

➥ And when you are attacked by cats and serpents in the dream, these are witchcraft attacks from the bottom of the pit.

➥ If the serpent is biting you in the dream, it is not a thing to take lightly. And if you see serpents in your dream and you fail to kill it, you should know for sure that the serpent is coming back to fight another day. So if you see yourself being pursued or bitten by serpents, the enemy is poisoning your life.

➥ See crocodile in the dream is bad because it is the spirit of the leviathan, the spirit that can disturb you emotionally, mentally and physically.

## Your Foundation and Your Destiny

➡ If you find yourself being flogged in the dream, this is an attempt to destroy your reputation.

➡ If you find yourself losing money in the dream, this is an attack on your finance.

➡ If you find somebody issuing curses on you in the dream, it means that forces of affliction and oppression are pursuing your life.

➡ If you find yourself bleeding through the nose or any other part of the body, this is witchcraft attack against your health.

➡ When you find yourself in the marketplace where sometimes you buy things and other times you don't, the enemy is trying to enslave you, and if you are not careful, they can give you mental disturbance.

➡ If you find yourself having sex in the dream, this is a sign that you have a spirit spouse.

➡ If you find yourself going back to your childhood days, it means the enemy wants to introduce retardation and backwardness into your life.

➡ If you find yourself dying in the dream or seeing coffin, this could mean death in various ways: financial, marital, spiritual. It may not necessarily mean that the person will die physically, these other things may die.

➡ Animals in the dream represent difficulties and problems, so if you see yourself being pursued in the dream by animals, it means problems are being introduced into the life of the person. And it is even worse when these animals do attack. For instance, when you see bats and owls in your dream, it means hypocrites are working against you and the spirit and forces of the night are also pursuing you.

➡ If you see yourself drinking alcohol in the dream, this represents confusion.

➡ If you see yourself with brooms, it means you are going to have friends who are not united.

➡ Seeing corpses in the dream are the forces of death coming into the person's life.

➡ If you see cobwebs in your dreams, this is the spirit of rejection and disfavour.

➡ If you find yourself wearing wigs in the dream, this is an evidence of fake glory.

➡ If you find yourself handcuffed in the dream, it means the enemy is putting his curse on your labour.

➡ If you find yourself with crabs, it means the enemy wants to introduce reversal into your life.

➡ When you find yourself roaming in the jungle, the enemy wants to make you sweat and gather nothing.

➡ If you keep seeing padlocks, it means that certain areas of your life have been locked up.

➡ If you dream and see chains, this means a very serious trap is being set for you.

➡ If you keep finding yourself always exhausted, it means the enemy is introducing fruitless struggles into your life.

➡ If you find yourself vomiting in the dream, it means the enemy is trying to make you lose your virtue.

➡ If you find yourself always crying in the dream, it means that the enemy is planning serious sorrow for your life.

➡ If you find yourself with rotten fruits or eggs in the dream, it means the enemy is introducing failure into your life.

Some people would notice that whenever they are about to do anything that would give them a major breakthrough, a particular dream would occur and when they have this dream, that is the end of the breakthrough.

# SOLUTION

The bottom line of it all, beloved, is this: if the enemy is attacking your destiny, your dream will show you that you are under attack. And in that situation what should you do?

*Complete dedication and consecration of your life to the Lord.* This means yielding everything about your life to the Lord, totally. Once this is done, the enemy cannot bewitch you.

When a lot of people come to MFM their enemies follow them and I have been cautioning and warning people that anytime they are coming here they should know that they are coming to the war front so that immediately they arrived from their vehicles they should start praying as the enemy is not happy that they are coming here.

*You must not be a satanic broadcasting station.* Who are satanic broadcasters? They are the gossips. When you come to our prayer meeting simply, face what you have come here to do. Men and women who lifted mountains

[173]

for God were those who learnt to be quiet; they were not talkative. A talkative cannot become a prophet.

*You must pray for the anointing of the Holy Spirit to fall upon you.* When this power falls upon you, things will change. The kind of Holy Ghost baptisms that people receive these days that sends things running after them needs to be checked.

That is why most of the churches that are moving the hand of God these days are pastored by men of God who got born again in the 70's. That time, when people received the baptism of the Holy Ghost, they knew that they received something as everything about them – dream life and what have you – changed, and those things that should have been running after them began to run away from them! These people received the real baptism of fire. You must pray for same to fall upon you.

*You must pray anti-dream attack prayers* that will barricade your dreams by fire so that you don't start dreaming what you should not dream.

*You must be completely holy.* Your level of holiness will determine how far the enemy will go in your life.

As I once said, once you consecrate your life and you pray, anointing will come upon you. When that anointing comes upon you it will produce revelations. When you now have the revelation, this will produce direction, and when you have direction success is bound to follow.

At this point, if it happens that you have one or two things to sort out with God, you can take the following prayer points. "Whatsoever is strengthening the enemy against me, whatsoever is turning my dream life to a battle field, Lord forgive me today; I want to rise by Your power, I want to move by Your strength; I want Your anointing to be upon me; I want Your glory to fill my life. Thank You, Jesus."

## PRAYER POINTS

1. Every satanic bondage programmed into my destiny, scatter, in the name of Jesus.

2. Every dream of failure in my past, die, in the name of Jesus.

3. Every witchcraft caterer pursuing my destiny, die, in the name of Jesus.

4. Every satanic dream attached to my progress, die, in the name of Jesus.

5. Every dream prison, break, in the name of Jesus;

6. I fire back every arrow of witchcraft fired into my dream, in the name of Jesus.

7. Every destiny demoting dream, die, in the name of Jesus;

8. Every dream of the past affecting my life now, die, in the name of Jesus.

9. Every witchcraft and serpent, what are you waiting for, die in the name of Jesus.

10. Every arrow fired against my marriage in the dream, die, in the name of Jesus.

11. (Lay your right hand on your head) Every mask of darkness working against my destiny, die in the name of Jesus.

12. Every power that says I shall not have peace, fall down and die, in the name of Jesus.

# THE MARKET SQUARE OF LIFE

***When*** Jesus was nailed on the cross there were all classes of people present.

First, we had the soldiers who nailed Him to the cross. They were there on official duty. Even if they did not agree that Jesus had to die, they just had to carry out the instruction given to them. This is because, being soldiers, they were duty-bound to obey the instructions of their superiors.

Another group of people present was thieves – one each on both sides of Jesus Christ there on the cross. One of them who was in trouble was even mocking Jesus. But the other said, "Remember me."

There also were those disciples of Christ who were bold enough to be there. Though they stood afar off, they were there all the same. Most of them had been with Jesus about three and a half years, yet there they were at that critical moment – too afraid to identify with Him.

There also were the innocent spectators who came to enjoy the spectacle reminiscent of the Roman one-man firing squad, but they did not know that they were watching the Prince of Peace being crucified. That is one of the reasons Jesus said, "They don't know what they are doing."

There also were people there like the Centurion who watched everything happening, at the end of which all he could say was, "Certainly, this man is a Son of God." All the same, he did not do much to salvage the situation.

There also was Mary, the mother of Jesus, as well as Mary Magdalene and other women who were quite close to Jesus.

There was also a man called Joseph of Arimathea, a secret disciple who eventually asked to bury the corpse of Jesus.

We had the chief priest, the scribes and the Pharisees who kept shouting, "Crucify Him, crucify Him; He trusted in God – let that God deliver Him now!"

All kinds of people were present at the cross but only a few understood the depth or implications of what was going on. That is why it is said that people who look are common but those who see are not common.

Thus, many have become, like the words of the street magician, "The more you look, the less you see; and the less you see, the less you understand; and the less you understand, the more foolish you become."

The man was saying all these things in the market place.

## <u>Your Foundation and Your Destiny</u>

All of us, without exception, are in the market square of life. Some know what they want but, unfortunately, many do not really know what they want, age notwithstanding.

They say a fool at forty is a fool forever. Of course, if you remain a fool at twenty-one you stand the risk of remaining a fool at forty. If you are a woman and you a fool at eighteen, you had better stop being a fool because you are not likely to recover from that state.

There are many confused people in the market square of life. The devil brings so many things to so many people, drag them to the market square and try to distract and confuse them. The enemy has headquarters in the market square of life where they try to confuse people. Herein, beloved, lies the problem in the life of the whole human race.

A lot of people are in the market square of life not really knowing what they want. Some are not even sure what they are doing there.

**In 1976,** while I was teaching a school lesson, there was a particular girl who used to sit in the front. Normally, when a teacher is writing, everyone is busy writing as well. But I noticed that this girl never wrote anything- she would just be staring at the chalk board. Even when asked to write something she would promise to write later. One day, the Lord said I was looking at almost a principality.

The job of a teacher is not a very easy one. Part of their occupational hazards is that they are teaching all kinds of strange people with strange eyes and strange ears. So I told this girl to see me after the class. When she met me after class, I told her straightway,

"You are possessed."

She confirmed this and said further that she had been to the world thirteen times. She said that when she came the twelfth time, it was through one woman by the side of their house. She went further to tell me strange stories about familiar spirits. She said that there is their evil kingdom where they had a grand-mother who, whenever anybody wanted to come to the world, would ask them,

"Do you want to go and trade?"

If anyone chose trading, she would instantly start the trade. I asked her what the 'trading' was all about. She laughed and said,

"We are traders."

Then I asked her that if she was a trader what then brought her to school? Again, she laughed heartily. At last, she told me,

[181]

"We trade in the souls of men."

It was at this point that the Scripture in Revelation made sense to me:

Rev. 18:11-13: And the merchants of the earth shall weep and mourn over her; for no man buyeth their merchandise any more: [12]The merchandise of gold, and silver, and precious stones, and of pearls, and fine linen, and purple, and silk, and scarlet, and all thyine wood, and all manner vessels of ivory, and all manner vessels of most precious wood, and of brass, and iron, and marble, [13]And cinnamon, and odours, and ointments, and frankincense, and wine, and oil, and fine flour, and wheat, and beasts, and sheep, and horses, and chariots, and slaves, and souls of men.

There are many gathered in the house of God day by day, who do not really know what life has for them. Many have already been confused and diverted. You need to use words today, as in the days before, to reposition yourself with prayer if the enemy has dislodged you from your rightful position.

The fact that you have money and you are doing very well does not mean that you are in position. The fact that you are single or married does not mean that you are in your divine position.

# SUCCESS KEYS IN THE MARKET SQUARE OF LIFE

Now, what do you do? What are the keys to the success in the market square of life?

### ➡ *Locate your divine position.*

Beloved, whether you believe it or not, you are here in this world to fulfil a divine agenda. You are not here for the enemy to be pushing you around. You are on a mission to accomplish a divine intention. You were created for this purpose and it is your responsibility to discover what you are supposed to do on the surface of the earth. It is your duty to find out your placement in life.

There is a great value that God has attached to you. God does not send anybody into the world just to roam about, or to be messed up. He has planted something in you to display to the world. It is your duty to search for this, find it and display it.

Every man who does not know where God has fitted him will definitely lose focus and when a man loses focus, he will collect his salary advance of backwardness and frustration. The moment you now discover your appointed place, your destiny will explode, things will now begin to open.

[183]

The knowledge of your position in life determines your progress. This is a serious matter.

### ➤ Know what God wants you to do

Some are doing so many things that God did not ask them to do.

> Then the word of the LORD came unto me, saying, before I formed thee in the belly I knew thee; and before thou camest forth out of the womb I sanctified thee, *and* I ordained thee a prophet unto the nations (Jeremiah 1:4-5).

There are so many people roaming about not knowing what to do. Many are even in the churches who need to pray themselves into position, pray themselves out of satanic schedule and reposition themselves in the schedule of God for their lives.

The above verse shows us how God operates. Before our fathers met our mothers, He had known us; and when we were in the womb He had decided what we should do here on earth. But the problem of man comes when he now arrives and begins acting contrary to God's plans and instructions.

For instance, since Jeremiah had been destined to be a prophet there could not have been prosperity for him in any other profession. In this same way, for as long as a man keeps working against God's plan for his life, he cannot expect to make any head-way. Such a person may go for deliverance and get some temporary relief but very soon the principle of destiny will come in to push him to where he should belong.

I was at home one day when I got a call from somebody who complained of difficulty in returning to his native country Nigeria, in spite of his wish. The fellow called from America. I simply told him to start coming home. He wondered if I understood what he was saying. He said he had been in America a long while and wanted to stay.

I never heard from him again until a long time after this, when he phoned to say he had now found a woman who wanted to marry him, but that it was an arranged marriage for which he would have to pay the woman. It was to facilitate his permanent stay in America! I advised that he should not do that, and should come home but he rebuffed my suggestion.

Then I asked him,

"Is it compulsory for you to stay in America?"

He said, well, he had been there for a long while. I did not hear from him for a long time again, until he phoned me for the third time to say that he needed prayers as the woman he was having the marriage of convenience with was giving him a headache. I asked what the headache was. He said the woman had refused to sign the papers unless he slept with her, which was never their arrangement, as he had previously told her all he wanted was the resident permit and nothing else.

I asked him where he had his own wife. He said the woman was in Nigeria. Then I asked him not to sleep with the woman in America but should come home. Still, he refused. He later turned to another minister there in America for counselling.

This meant he was not pleased with my suggestion to him. It is for this reason that someone once remarked that if you take an usher to America from Nigeria, he will become a bishop there. The minister in America simply asked the man to go ahead and sleep with the woman and then ask for forgiveness from God later.

So, the brother went ahead to sleep with the woman, not knowing that she had H. I. V. The brother died shortly afterwards. That marked the end of his destiny, terminated by the enemy in the middle of his life! May this never be your lot, in Jesus' name.

It is important for you to pray to God to show you your appointed place in life. It may be the reason for the poverty you are currently experiencing. Certainly, if prophet Jeremiah decided to go and become a medical doctor I am sure he would have killed all his patients and he would have been arrested because his drugs would fail to work as he had been ordained to be nothing besides a prophet.

Abraham was raised up to plant the nation Israel.

Joseph was raised up to preserve life.

Moses was raised up as a deliverer.

Joshua was raised up to lead the people to the promised land.

Paul was raised up as an apostle to the Gentiles.

All these men just focussed on what they were supposed to do.

The question now is: what were you raised up to do?

You need to find out what God has called you to do. It may take you five minutes' prayer, or even ten minutes or one hour, or a month, you must find it out and focus on that assignment, give it all you have then your journey for attainment will start.

A brother got born again. His father was the owner of the largest alcohol company in that country. When the father died, the brother inherited the company. He then went to a preacher to say that when his father was selling alcohol he saw, many times, so many women coming to the front of their house crying and begging the family to stop selling alcohol to their husbands, as alcohol had ruined their homes. On many occasions, he said, his father would kick these women away.

For this, the young man now asked the preacher to help pray for his forgiveness. The preacher assured him that God would forgive him, but only if he would close down the multi-million dollar business. And the brother said, "So shall it be." Thus, he closed it down so as to locate himself into what God wanted him to do.

It is necessary for you to find out what God wants you to do. If you should fail to find out, you will still be like those who were at the cross and saw one man, one funny man like that crying, "God why hath thou forsaken me?" You will be exactly like this man who all he saw was this, whereas someone else saw the man and said, "Surely, this is the Son of God."

A lot of us are in that market square. We pray all kinds of prayers from morning till night, which is not bad in itself; but there would have been no prayer point that would have helped Jeremiah if he had decided not to be a prophet.

While I was a student at the University of Lagos, we had a boy in our class who never copied notes. We never found him reading and anytime he saw us sweating over our books he would be smiling and telling us, "It is easier to read your book under the water." We wondered what this meant. At that time I was a foolish Christian even though I had been born again and received the baptism of the Holy Ghost. All the boy said turned out to be ploys meant to divert our attention from our books.

When a person misses his way in the journey of life, he will find himself in the gutter of life. When the enemy diverts your attention and you allow him to do it, he will surely destroy you.

Just what are we saying here?

There is something many people call the spirit of man. That thing knows you more than you know yourself and generally wants you to do the right thing.

This makes most people want to do the right thing but then they are faced with diversionary forces. When you shift from the calling of God for your life, your problem in life begins. Diversion will rend your destiny and it will end it all in frustration.

Sister Bolus was meant to be one of the best female pilots. The enemy knew this. Right inside the lady's heart, she too wanted to become a pilot but then the forces of diversion started working on her at a very young age. The enemy gave her destiny-demoting friends. I pray that any friend that is demoting your destiny will depart from you in the name of Jesus.

Those friends kept telling her to do something about her flat breasts. She asked what she could do. They advised her to get a boyfriend. They subsequently mounted pressure on her until she went out to pick a boy friend.

You can say anything about the devil and call him any name you like, but, you cannot call him a fool. Indeed, if you look at his strategies in the Bible, you will find he is a very intelligent creature. He knows our tastes, likes and dislikes, strengths and weaknesses, and he plans his strategies around these.

When the devil wanted to deal with Joseph he went and picked the most beautiful woman around to start harassing him. It was the same case with sister Bolus. The enemy went and picked a boyfriend for her from a blood-sucking family. After meeting the man just once, she got pregnant and gave birth to a triplet. This stopped her education. She got confined to her home and had a caesarian operation. All the three babies died. Though she went back to school, she was never the same again.

All those friends who advised her have gone ahead now. And every time she slept now, there would be the cries of these babies. It was as if she was running mad. The enemy had thrown a spanner into the wheel of her destiny. Now, she is a clothes dealer. What a diversion!

Any diversion of your destiny will lead you to the wilderness of regret. What many old people call experience is often an exercise in regrets. The enemy rings multiple bells in our ears to get our attention; he shows glittering things to divert our attention.

While working as a research officer in 1988, I went to the University of Paris for research. Right there on the underground train, I found someone looking like a Nigerian. He spoke to me in Yoruba, and since I had not seen anyone to talk to in my native language for sometime, I sat down to talk with him there. Curiously, I discovered he was always looking backward and forward.

All of a sudden, there emerged a policeman from the other end. When the policeman saw both of us discussing, he said, in French, "Please, . . ." Immediately, the young man took off. I was amazed. The policeman came to where I sat and spoke in French. I told him I could not comprehend what he was saying.

Then came another policeman who could speak English. This new one asked me who I was and what I was doing where I was. They asked me to show them my immigration papers. Since I had none on me I showed them my laboratory papers and other related documents on me. They still could not believe what I was telling them until I brought a note from my laboratory. It was then they apologised and let me go.

I later met the young Nigerian who ran away and asked why he did so. He said he had no paper. Then I asked him why he preferred that running around to staying in one place to rest. He said he just had to get something. But I wondered what he was really getting with all the trouble. The answer was: plain diversion!

The enemy paints the road in gold in order to make you follow that path to destruction. Unfortunately, you cannot fly like an eagle when your employer is a turkey because you will be looking in the wrong place.

The enemy gets the attention of so many people and leads them to the stream of unfulfilled destiny.

The devil is also an expert at making immediate alternative provisions so that when he wants you to leave your own destiny, he quickly makes an alternative arrangement not meant for you. He engages your attention with counterfeit goals in order to mislead you for life. If it were a temporary thing, it would have been no problem but, unfortunately, beloved, one minute of absence from

## Your Foundation and Your Destiny

your divinely designated post can cause a damage that may not be repaired in your life time.

The enemy has a lot of broadcasters around. This makes it important for Christians to control what they hear because what you hear determines what you feel. What you feel decides what you fear, and what you fear determines how far you will go in life.

If you have anyone telling you what does not increase your faith, run! If all that the person says to you are gossips, slander and backbiting, run! Such a person is sure to divert your destiny.

Anything that is going to enter into your ears must first be screened, and if it is not faith-building, you have the right to reject it because, when the enemy begins to put information into your ears, it will soon go into your heart, and the Bible says, "Finally, brethren, whatsoever things are pure, whatsoever things are lovely, whatsoever things are of good report, think of these things."

Once the enemy takes you away from those things, he is diverting you. That is why I always advise people to have only good friends whichever Church they go to and not friends who will pull them down. You must have just those friends who will speak challenging words into your ears and make you go home challenged; not friends who will speak to you and after you have gone away, would start mocking you. This kind of thing hardly increases anyone's faith.

If you come across someone who always speaks the words of defeat, you had better run from him or her because, very soon, he or she will divert you.

If someone keeps talking of something that will make you fall into sin, run, because very soon, he will divert your destiny, and after he has diverted it, and your life is wasted, a man of God will one day take an altar call and the person who had diverted your destiny will come forward to repent for telling you lies that wasted your life, and the Lord will forgive that person. But, meanwhile, you are already in trouble.

It is like the case of Jesus of Agege who prophesied in 1940 that Lagos would sink under the sea. After the man had deceived so many people, he declared himself born again. And the mystery of our faith is that God would forgive him but those people who listened to him are already finished.

There was once a fellow in Ajegunle who called himself the 'Holy Spirit'. He had a congregation. Sooner or later he too got born again but all those who attended his church are hell-bound.

### ➡ *Wrong habits and attitudes must die.*

If you do not want to roam in the market square of life, wrong habits and wrong attitudes must die. You must remove all these out of your life. The Bible says that you must remove yourself from those sins that easily beset you. It also says, "Let all that call the name of the Lord depart from iniquity."

If you must be the person God wants you to be, your tongue must be bridled and sanctified.

The tongue is a good way of knowing the kind of person one is dealing with. If you are an advertiser or an example of a leaking tongue, you will not make it in life. The power of God will not rest mightily on you if you are talkative.

If you must be a giant in the field of destiny success, you must be a person of few essential words. If you must be an oracle of God, speak only when the Holy Ghost speaks. Let the Spirit of God in your life get into gear before you start to talk with your mouth.

The habit of loose tongue must die.

Lying is an attitude that pulls down success. All liars will never attain excellence.

I may well ask you a question here: When last did you tell a lie? When last did you gossip or backbite? Some people can only tell the truth at the point of death. It is at that point they confess their sins and ask their pastor to pray for them.

The tongue is a signpost of a man's life and heavens take note of every idle word so that if you tell lies or you happen to be a liar, you end up in the dustbin of sorrow. And any falsehood in your life is a sure way of deceiving your destiny.

If your life is taken over by any sin, you will be digging your own pit if you do not identify this sin and deal with it.

If you want to overcome in the market square of life you must find out the sin that so easily besets you and remove it.

If you do not know what your weaknesses are you are in a serious trouble. You must find out what your weaknesses are and correct them. That sin that you are petting and pampering, that sin you are craving for are strategies to destroy your destiny. You have to identify your weaknesses and deal with them.

I have once shared the story of a man who was coming out of a brothel as I was passing through Ojuelegba one day. Right at the door of a prostitute he lifted up his voice and sang, "It is well, it is well, with my soul, with my soul . . ."

## Your Foundation and Your Destiny

The fact that the man knew that song showed that there was a touch of God upon his life. This made him rejoice that it was well with his soul while he should have been dealing with the wrong habit in his life.

At the point you have to tell God to come into you now to help you see if there is any sin or wickedness in you.

What is it that the enemy sees and rejoices? Is there anything in your life that you need to correct so that you can move forward?

It is good for you to examine yourself now so that you can start to make amends.

Learn to identify your weaknesses and deal with them. Ask yourself questions: Is there indiscipline in my life?

We need discipline to read the Bible. We need disciple to pray, fast and evangelise.

Is there impatience in your life? Are you head-strong? Do people anger you easily? Are you a student in the school of worry? Are you too sensitive? Are you very doubtful? Are you inconsistent? Are you fearful? Do you have any bitterness against anybody in your heart?

Are you argumentative? Are you domineering? Are you unforgiving? Are you talkative? Or are you lazy? Are you too loud? Are you always critical?

Ask yourself these questions with a view to identifying your weaknesses and when you have found them, do not let them rest. If you leave them there to rest, it is like you are leaving the enemy to go unmolested. Identify your sins, deal with them. Do not use the gradual approach. Nobody asked you to manage anger or pride – they just must go or die and be replaced with a life devoted to God.

➡ *Let your problem become your promotion.*

Everybody has an enemy. If you feel that you do not have an enemy it means you have the greatest enemy and he has blinded you from seeing him.

Every man is even entitled to an enemy because opposition prepares one for one's miracle. If you are looking for people without enemies the best place to go is the cemetery. Even if you think you do not have enemies you had better apply to heaven to give you one because your enemy will reveal to you the state of your heart, your wickedness and the weakness in your won spirit.

Many people did not believe that they could smash the head of another person until the enemy decides to abuse them. When people feel that they do not have enemies they feel they are perfect as they are but under intense pressure from their enemy, they do the unthinkable.

## Your Foundation and Your Destiny

A sister once told me that she had to grab the guitar from a man who was talking rubbish to her and smashed it on his head. This made the man also to get up, seize the woman's newly bought televison set and smash it on the floor. Then a real fight began. This was a couple that got married in the church.

We grow through challenges and problems. If you are a pastor, you need an elder who will be harassing you and attacking you so that you can go on your knees and pray.

If you are a student, you must have that lecturer who does not like to see your face and, in the process, make you get serious and read hard to improve yourself.

As a teacher you need that student who will constantly be telling you that what you write is wrong so that you too can grow.

We all need these oppositions; they make us kneel down and pray.

MFM has so many enemies. To tell the truth, we thank them most sincerely. They are part of our moving forces. If anyone is busy criticising MFM, he or she is doing a very good job because he or she is making us to move forward. Many people would not have known about the Mountain of Fire and Miracles Ministries at all if their pastors had not been preaching against MFM as a demonic place not to be given any attention. Then those who feel like having a feel of this strange place eventually make their way to MFM, and get struck with the wonders taking place there, never wanting to go elsewhere again.

So, even though these other people criticise us, they help to move us forward. When MFM started in Abuja, I was going there every Tuesday for almost one year. Little did I know that we were annoying some pastors. Before MFM started in Abuja, some churches were running three shifts but by the time we got in, the three shifts reduced to half shifts – the people just moved. This angered some pastors who went to report me that I was stealing people. I was maliciously accused of anti-government activities. This made the government to plant its agents in our church there, to constantly monitor and record our services.

However, at an altar call one Sunday, the first person to come out was the very person detailed to monitor us! Many other successes we have recorded would have been impossible without opposition.

There are some places where they do not even know MFM at all until somebody wrote a petition against us as 'thousands of people' making noise. This only brought people to come and see such noisy multitude. And when they came, they sat down.

Problems help you to identify your weak areas. They help you to fortify your walls of defence.

Problems help you to solidify your strategies of attack and help you to rebuild your internal character.

Problems help you to be humble and depend completely on God and not on your brain.

For instance, when a man goes to see a doctor with an ailment and the doctor asks him to say his last prayer because there is no way out of his ailment, where does such a person turn to if not God?

When you talk to human beings about your problem, they always have their own definition. Anything that works against a person's comfort is a problem. They are right. Indeed, anything that works against anyone's joy is a problem.

But in God's book, His own definition is different. To God, a problem is an opportunity for Him to prove His power, an opportunity wearing work clothes.

To God, it is an opportunity to manifest His ability and display His Almightiness.

To God, a problem is a way of producing a fence of dependence on Him, a way of proving His integrity.

[201]

To God, a problem is an opportunity to promote us to higher heights.

The times of trouble are the only times God is able to get our attention. It is for this reason that God some times uses the enemy. And that is how we have been able to develop the prayer point: My problem shall become my promotion.

If you feel that your husband or your wife is wicked, let the wickedness turn you to a prayer warrior. Your problems can become crutches for you to walk with, or wings for you to soar high.

### ➡ *Persistence*.

The book of Mark 10:46-52:

And they came to Jericho: and as he went out of Jericho with his disciples and a great number of people, blind Bartimaeus, the son of Timaeus, sat by the highway side begging. [47]And when he heard that it was Jesus of Nazareth, he began to cry out, and say, Jesus, *thou* Son of David, have mercy on me. [48]And many charged him that he should hold his peace: but he cried the more a great deal, *Thou* Son of David, have mercy on me. [49]And Jesus stood still, and commanded him to be called. And they call the blind man, saying unto him, Be of good comfort, rise; he calleth thee. [50]And he, casting away his garment, rose, and came to Jesus. [51]And Jesus answered and said unto him, What wilt thou that I should do unto thee? The blind man said unto him, Lord, that I might receive my sight. [52]And Jesus said unto him, Go thy way; thy faith hath made thee whole. And immediately he received his sight, and followed Jesus in the way.

In the above passage we meet the blind Bartimeaus who had a problem and knew that he had a problem. He knew the fellow could solve it and so began to cry unto Jesus.

Many, who had him, shouted him down to hold his peace and die in his blindness, but he cried the more. Which means that those people shouting him down only succeeded in making him increase his volume, and due to the persistence of this man, Jesus gave him attention and healed him.

What does it mean to persist?

It means to be stubbornly repetitious, to be insistent.

To be persistent is to hold firm and steadfastly to one purpose despite discouragement, obstacles and setbacks.

It is to refuse to stop, to persevere, to be fixed, to remain unmoved – this is persistence.

Unfortunately, this is one character that is fast getting out of the life of the modern man.

Blind Bartimeaus was a classic example of persistence over-coming resistance. Persistence is to insist on your goal, and nothing in life can take the place of persistence.

## Your Foundation and Your Destiny

If, when Bartimaeus was shouted down, he just kept his peace, and did not persist, he would have died blind.

There are many talented men and women in our environment but who are failures because of lack of persistence. This lack of persistence has dragged so many men and women into the valley of defeat.

There was a man who, though an unbeliever, challenged my life as a Christian.

While in the university many years ago, a panel was set up before which every student was asked to appear with the originals of their certificates. The first time this order was given everybody laughed it off as a huge joke. They could not imagine how anyone could come to the university without a certificate.

However, by the next morning, the lecture room was almost bare of students. This was unbelievable. It means that so many students actually did not have the required papers to be in the university. Then there was this man who got into the university at the age of thirty-two. By age thirty-six he had got to his final year. And because everyone who came into the university with a forged certificate had run away, he too ran away. He had a false certificate. But he never gave up. At that age of thirty-six he went back to sit for the secondary school certificate examination he had escaped from. And by the time he was thirty-eight he was back again in year one in the university. And by fort- one or two he got the degree. The man is now doing impressively well in the society.

To a majority of human beings, however, an end would have been put to their efforts at that point the man ran away from the university. And there are so many reasons to give up one of which is the question:

"How can it be heard that I will come and sit in the class again?" And that would have paralysed the man's destiny. This has pulled a lot of people in the valley of defeat.

Sometimes, when some people are advised to go and repeat their exams in the same school, it sounds repulsive to them to sit down with their juniors, thus remaining in that valley of defeat. This can be very sad.

The story of that man challenged me even as a Christian. His fighting spirit was something else. We need to wake up from the slumber of allowing the enemy to just dump us in the valley and remain there.

Sometimes, when some people are given some scriptures to memorise, even at the age of forty-eight, they would say that their brain is not good enough to hold any scripture. This is the evidence of defeat.

*Now, what are the enemies of persistence?*

*Lack of purpose*: You cannot be persistent without a purpose. Without a goal from God, you cannot pray when the hard time comes because you do not really know what He wants you to do.

Several years back, a sister prayed when a brother proposed marriage to her. God said it was her match but that for the first ten years of this marriage she would suffer like no man's business, but that, thereafter, He would prosper her husband.

So the sister went into the affair. Those ten years, truly, turned out to be a terrible period. So bad were things that they would put gari in water while the children were crying to eat and let the gari swell up in the water to be sufficient for the family. At a point the sister wanted to give up under pressure from members of her family. And at that time, other men, rich and good looking, began to come to propose to the sister. Then she remembered what the Lord told her. This made her to persist. She is now enjoying.

Without a purpose, we really cannot persist. Lack of purpose is an enemy of persistence.

One white man once remarked that a man would work eight hours a day for a pay; a man would work for ten hours a day for a good bus, but a man can work for twenty-four hours a day for a good course when he knows that a good is coming to him from it. The first enemy of persistence is lack of focus.

Bartimaeus heard that Jesus was passing and knew that the Man had the power to heal him so he pursued that purpose. I pray that the spirit that gives up will not come upon your life, in the name of Jesus.

A lot of people give up on prayer after some efforts. Such people are only courting trouble because, at that point where they give up, they may be very close to a breakthrough. So, giving up at that point is like taking three steps forward and taking other five steps backward.

*Making excuses is the second enemy of persistence*. And they say an excuse is a gathered lie. Excuses mean looking for exit signs, and it is responsible for ninety-nine percent of all the failures that we find around us.

Moses gave tons and tons of excuses why God could not use him.

Jeremiah, too, gave excuses, but God said, "Keep quiet, do what I asked you to do."

*Dodging one's responsibility*. When God said, Adam, where art thou?" Adam said, "I was in the garden but I was afraid." The Lord asked him if he had eaten of the forbidden fruit, and Adam began to blame the devil and Eve, just like Sarah blamed Hagar. Persisters, on the other hand, accept and face their responsibility.

*Lack of stamina.* This is the inability to stick to a course of action for a while. This is another enemy of persistence.

*Laziness.* When we are looking for lazy Christians, today's Christians rank tops. They are too lazy to pray, read the Bible, witness and even fast.

*Lack of determination.* A person who lacks determination is certain to stagnate.

*Listening to failures is another enemy of persistence.* You need to close your ears to anything that you hear and does not add to your faith.

Persistence does not recognise any limitation.

Persistence treats life's problems like onions – it removes them layer by layer. Deliverance, too, is like that. As you remove one layer you come to another one and remove that one too until you get to the last one. Many are ignorant of this.

When you mix your persistence with determination you will succeed.

*Seek and receive divine information.*

# Your Foundation and Your Destiny

In the book of Job 29:4-9 we read:

As I was in the days of my youth, when the secret of God *was* upon my tabernacle; ⁵When the Almighty *was* yet with me, *when* my children *were* about me; ⁶When I washed my steps with butter, and the rock poured me out rivers of oil; ⁷When I went out to the gate through the city, *when* I prepared my seat in the street! ⁸The young men saw me, and hid themselves: and the aged arose, *and* stood up. ⁹The princes refrained talking, and laid *their* hand on their mouth.

And verse 25 says:

I chose out their way, and sat chief, and dwelt as a king in the army, as one *that* comforteth the mourners.

How was Job able to achieve all this? This takes us back to verse 4:

As I was in the days of my youth, when the secret of God was upon my tabernacle . . .

The secret of God was upon Job's tabernacle.

Power is to have access into the mystery of God.

Power is to have access to the mystery of the Kingdom.

Power is to have access into the mystery of the world. Mystery is undisclosed treasure, something that is hidden. The wisdom of God is hidden. You must, therefore, ask God to grant you access into the mystery of life. Because the mystery of God was upon the tabernacle of Job, when the secret of life was upon his life, he washed his hands with butter while others used ordinary water. When young men saw him they just disappeared; when the old people saw him, they rose up to greet him, even princes stopped talking at his approach and the nobles held their peace, their tongue cleaved to the roof of their mouth. He was the one who decided for them, according to verse 25.

Beloved, you need access into the mysteries of life, into the mystery of the word of God. We need access into the Kingdom of God. All those things that we do in life have secrets: business, marriage, every problem or profession.

I once read the story of the beginning of Coca-Cola. It was said that one young man went there and told them that he would teach them something that would make the product sell very well but that they must promise to give him 50 cents from every bottle they sold. They asked him what the secret was and he told them to start putting the drink inside bottles. Initially, they baulked at the suggestion but eventually decided to give it a trial. Up till today, the man is still collecting his 50 cents per bottle of Coke sold.

If you have been struggling for years inside a profession without success, have you asked to know what the secret of that profession is?

A sister who was well-advanced in age found it difficult to get a husband despite her ravishing beauty. At the peak of her desperation, she met a man of God who gave her some prayer points bordering on spirit husband.

After being handed the prayer points, the sister resolved to know the beneficial secret that would move her life forward, so she prayed with a holy anger. Afterwards, she fell asleep during which she dreamt of being in a big church with lots of people in attendance and she was at the altar where she was being married to a man. Presiding over the whole affair was a pastor. Everything went on smoothly up till the point where she was asked,

"Will you take . . . to be your husband..."

It was at this point that the sister looked up to see the face of the man she was being wedded to and found it was none other than her father's.

"Abomination!" She protested. But this did not impress the officiating pastor who insisted that abomination or not, the wedding must go on. At this point, the sister woke up from her sleep. She then ran to her father to tell him what she saw. All the man could say was,

"Well, you see . . ., you look like my grand mother . . . when you were to be born, we were told it was my grand mother coming back, and this explains why I always prostrate to you. Then, again, when your mother was on her death-bed, she entreated me not to marry any other wife but that I should take you as my wife . . ."

All this sounded strange to the sister, but she had no illusion about what she had to do: strange prayers that would set her free from every evil link with her own father, as well as every evil link with her mother.

This world is a deep, deep place but many are so naive that they think that the world is just a place of comedy, entertainment and merriment. It is not so. The more you pray about your life the more you discover.

Praying about your life will lead to discovery. When your prayers get to a level, deep secrets will be made known. You really need to raise your voice to the heavens because it is the truth that you know that can set you free.

It is a tragedy for you not to understand yourself. It is a tragedy for the enemy to come and say, "O. k., identify yourself..." It is a tragedy when you cannot identify yourself, or understand yourself. If your name were to be entered into a dictionary, it would be a tragedy if you would not know how to define yourself.

Perhaps, as you read this, you are already tired of it all and you are being overwhelmed by many life's challenges, and you have chronic financial problems and you can hardly understand what is going on in your life to the extent that you have lost touch with yourself.

Perhaps you seem to be a stranger even to your own self, and others too are looking at you like a total stranger. You definitely need to cry out to the Lord today to let you know the secret that will move you forward.

I have had to share before, the story of a boy called Yisa. He was the youngest boy in his family. As he was returning home from school one day, he saw a big woman sitting down by the gate. The woman's breasts were so long that they touched the ground. As the woman saw the young Yisa coming she said,

"My husband."

Shocked, the boy asked,

"Who are you?"

The woman replied,

"I'm your wife."

The boy just hissed and went inside the house. When he saw his father he told him of the woman she saw by the gate whose breasts touched the ground. He told his father how the woman called him his husband. The father began to cry saying,

"And I've been looking forward to this woman showing herself to me for years, and while she hid herself from me she has revealed herself to you."

The boy was surprised by all this strange talk.

"The woman you have just seen," the father told Yisa, "is the strongman of our family! All those who have seen her in the family are now rich people; I have never seen her, but you have just seen her."

This made Yisa to start rejoicing, not knowing that his problems had just started. By the time Yisa would discover himself, his life had been wrecked to a terrible level.

The major problem that people have is that they do not know themselves; they do not know what God wants them to know about themselves. And many times, people cannot do spiritual sharp-shooting because they just do not know what to shoot at. And, definitely, some breakthroughs will not come until a person discovers what to shoot at and begin to shoot it down.

A couple once came for prayer because their home had been turned to a battle ground. When they came, the Lord asked if I knew why they were fighting. I said no. The Lord then asked me to tell them to go and check their wedding present. Then I asked them if they had ever looked through all the wedding presents they received at their wedding. They had been married for five years and most of the presents they received that day were just put in a store; they never went there.

When I told them, they went home and brought out all unopened presents and began to open them. Then they got to a particular one with the skeleton of a big snake neatly wrapped in the gift box. The demonic snake had been with them for five odd years!

A final year student of mathematics was once brought to our church mad. She was all right before she went to bed, but the next day, she woke up stark mad. While the parents fretted and cried, the Lord told the pastor that the case needed no prayer. The pastor asked the Lord why and God said, "Simply ask the father of the girl to go to his own father: in the man's room there is a coffin buried there; tell him to bring out the coffin and open it and the girl will be well."

While the Lord spoke to the pastor, the father of the girl was still busy crying expecting the pastor to pray for the girl, but the pastor simply told the man what the Lord had said to him.

Fortunately, the man's father lived within same city. When he met the old man, the man told him about his daughter's condition.

Alarmed, the old man asked, "Have you taken her to the doctor?" The man said they had and that none could help them, hence they took the girl to a church for prayer. "And how much has that helped her?" The old man wanted to know. "They even say prayer is not what she needs to get well."

"But what?" asked the old man.

"And that is what has brought me here."

"And what is that?" asked the old man.

"The pastor says there is a coffin buried inside this room, that if it is exhumed Esua will get well."

The old man looked at his son with disbelief and, at last, asked him to describe the pastor who had just told him this. The description the man gave seemed to strike a recognition cord in his father's mind. "That pastor?" he asked, "I know him." The man thereafter went ahead to bring out the small coffin and opened it, after which the brother left.

By the time he got back to the church, his daughter was already drinking soft drinks, chatting and joking with everyone around. But then, without the disclosure of the truth about her background, her destiny would have been destroyed by a man who did not want to die on time and wanted to use Esua's life to continue his own.

There are many dead but walking people around. By God's arithmetic, they never showed up on earth. They are present, but absent. They are right here on earth, but they have not shown up. And, beloved, you never really meet real people. This is the truth. Most people you meet are people who became what they are because people said that is what they should be. Which means that most people are what others say they are, and not what God says they are.

Most people you meet are people who became what their parents said they should become, and not what God wanted them to become, some made themselves what they are by the enemy. This, in effect, means we meet few real people who came here and are doing exactly what God wanted them to do.

You need access to the mystery of God, as well as beneficial secrets about your life. If you do not have this secret, you will be completely ignorant of your divine destiny, then you possess this sense of selfishness, a sense of self-hatred, a sense of self-rejection, a feeling of being unwanted, or unneeded. As these prevail, the victims steadily withdraw into themselves. Even when such a person comes to church meetings, he wants to stay quietly by himself without talking to anybody.

[217]

When people do not know the secret, there would be this feeling of inadequacy which gets them busy coping and wanting to be like others. In the process, they become moody as they know deep inside them that they are not doing what they are supposed to do.

There is a department in the market square of life to where the enemy diverts people's lives so as to get them consumed in the battle of life.

The question is: Do you have the secrets that will help your life move forward?

Jeroboam was a terrible king who knew that God did not like him. He had a son that was dying. Nobody knew the secret of why that son was dying. For this, Jeroboam sent his wife to prophet Ahijah to find out for him whether that child would live.

1 Kings 14:1-13:

At that time Abijah the son of Jeroboam fell sick. ²And Jeroboam said to his wife, Arise, I pray thee, and disguise thyself, that thou be not known to be the wife of Jeroboam; and get thee to Shiloh: behold, there is Ahijah the prophet, which told me that *I should be* king over this people. ³And take with thee ten loaves, and cracknels, and a cruse of honey, and go to him: he shall tell thee what shall become of the child. ⁴And Jeroboam's wife did so, and arose, and went to Shiloh, and came to the house of Ahijah. But Ahijah could not see; for his eyes were set by reason of his age. ⁵And the LORD said unto Ahijah, Behold, the wife of Jeroboam cometh to ask a thing of thee for her son; for he is sick: thus and thus shalt thou say unto her: for it shall be, when she cometh in, that she shall feign herself *to be* another *woman*. ⁶And it was *so*, when Ahijah heard the sound of her feet as she came in at the door, that he said, Come in, thou wife of Jeroboam; why feignest thou thyself *to be* another? for I *am* sent to thee *with* heavy *tidings*. ⁷Go, tell Jeroboam, Thus saith the LORD God of Israel, Forasmuch as I exalted thee from among the people, and made thee prince over my people Israel, ⁸And rent the kingdom away from the house of David, and gave it thee: and yet thou hast not been as my servant David, who kept my commandments, and who followed me with all his heart, to do *that* only *which was* right in mine eyes; ⁹But hast done evil above all that were before thee: for thou hast gone and made thee other gods, and molten images, to provoke me to anger, and hast cast me behind thy back: ¹⁰Therefore, behold, I will bring evil upon the house of Jeroboam, and will cut off from Jeroboam him that pisseth against the wall, *and* him that is shut up and left in Israel, and will take away the remnant of the house of Jeroboam, as a man taketh away dung, till it be all gone. ¹¹Him that dieth of Jeroboam in the city shall the dogs eat; and him that dieth in the field shall the fowls of the air eat: for the LORD hath spoken it. ¹²Arise thou therefore, get thee to thine own house: *and* when thy feet enter into the city, the child shall die. ¹³And all Israel shall mourn for him, and bury him: for he only of Jeroboam shall come to the grave, because in him there is found *some* good thing toward the LORD God of Israel in the house of Jeroboam.

What God is telling us in the above passage is that only that child will come to the grave in the whole house of Jeroboam, because in him was found some good thing towards the Lord God of Israel. Which means that in the whole of Jeroboam's household, God just decided to remove only that boy so that he will not experience what the whole household would experience.

We need such divine information to move ahead in life.

We need divine information to make progress.

We need divine information where we are right now.

There is no where in the Bible that says you must do your business and fail.

There is nowhere in the Bible that says that, as a Christian, you must wear the garment of a debtor.

There is nowhere in the Bible that says the powers of darkness must pursue a child of God and defeat him.

There is nowhere in the Bible that says that evil will pursue righteousness and the evil will succeed.

There is nowhere in the Bible that says apostle so so and so will die because household witches and wizards will kill him.

There is nowhere in the Bible where men of God are classified as failures.

Therefore, you too are not supposed to fail; you are supposed to be a success. If you have been wrongly positioned, it is time to discover what you are really supposed to be doing. Perhaps you have been selling the wrong thing, making the wrong money, sleeping with the wrong partner, mixing with your enemies and warming yourself in the fire of the enemy; you need to pray with thunder and fire the following prayer points.

## PRAYER POINTS

1. O Lord, show me myself in my dream, in the name of Jesus.

2. O Lord, show me my divine position, in the name of Jesus.

3. O Lord, process my life into fulfilment, in Jesus name.

4. O Lord, make your way plain before my face, in the name of Jesus.

5. O Lord, if I am in the wrong schedule, reposition me, in the name of Jesus.

6. Every platform of failure prepared by my ancestors, I am not your candidate, in Jesus name.

7. Every satanic diversion of my destiny, die! in the name of Jesus.

8. Thou power of diversion working against my destiny, die in the name of Jesus.

9. (Lay your right hand on your head the other on your belly button). I close down every factory of the enemy in my life, in Jesus' name.

10. My placenta, my blood, reject destiny bewitchment, in the name of Jesus.

11. My problem shall become my promotion, in the name of Jesus.

12. I shall succeed, I shall not fail; failure is not in my blood, I locate myself into my position designed by God. I move forward by fire, in the name of Jesus.

13. Every power that wants my destiny to expire, it is you that will expire, in the name of Jesus.

14. I shall not give up; it is my problems that shall give up, in the name of Jesus.

15. Every power of parental witchcraft working against my destiny, die, in Jesus name.

16. (Lift up your right hand.) You that troubleth my Israel, my God shall trouble you, in the name of Jesus.

17. Power to persist until breakthrough, come upon my life now, in the name of Jesus.

18. Every secret the enemy is trying to hide from me, be revealed by fire, in Jesus' name.

19. Every serpent of destruction hiding in my destiny, die! in the name of Jesus.

20. Any power planning to shorten my life, what are you waiting for? die, in the name of Jesus.

21. Every foundation of spiritual blindness, break! in the name of Jesus.

22. O God, arise and show me myself, in the name of Jesus.

23. O Lord, arise and convert my dreams to revelations in the name of Jesus.

24. O God, give me divine creativity that will usher me into prosperity in the name of Jesus.

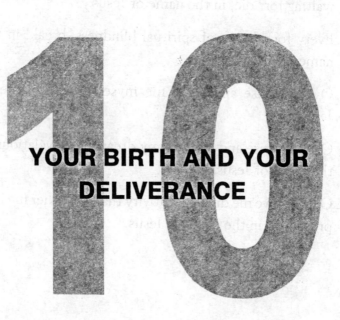

# YOUR BIRTH AND YOUR DELIVERANCE

# LIFE STARTS FROM THE WOMB

We shall start off this chapter by reading the book of Hebrews 7:9-10:

And as I may so say, Levi also, who receiveth tithes, payed tithes in Abraham. [10]For he was yet in the loins of his father, when Melchisedec met him.

There was a man called Levi. Abraham was not the direct father of Levi – Abraham gave birth to Isaac, then Isaac gave birth to Jacob, and Levi was one of the sons of Jacob.

We can see how far this fellow was from Levi. Now the Bible is saying that Levi was paying tithes inside the lions of Abraham.

Now, in Luke 1:15, says:

For he shall be great in the sight of the Lord, and shall drink neither wine nor strong drink; and he shall be filled with the Holy Ghost, even from his mother's womb.

The first verse has to do with Levi, who the Bible says even though he was yet to be born, was already paying tithes through the life of Abraham. And the second one talks about John the Baptist who had been filled with the Holy Ghost even from his mother's womb. These two passages are our working passages for this chapter.

[225]

## Your Foundation and Your Destiny

There is a popular game called rugby. Sometime ago, many people used to play football on village streets. When the game started, hundreds of men used to play it at one time, instead of the eleven-a-side that we have these days.

In those days, it could even be five-hundred-a-side. All they needed for the football was the blown bladder of an animal. This they kicked all over the place with all the men each trying to get his foot at it. This made the game very rough. It was a common sight, in those days, for people's clothes to be torn during a match. Even arms and legs did get broken.

There was a goal post at one end of town and another one at the other end. Only one rule applied then: get the ball into the opponent's goal post, regardless by what means this was done. At the end of the game, all the men who took part in it would be thoroughly dirty, smelly, some would have fallen into streams and ditches because, sometimes, between one goal post and the other lay rivers.

So rough and dirty was the game that a man who saw some British men playing it said, "If this is a game, I would hate to see British men fighting."

Then, later, schools began to play the game. With time, the number of participants got reduced. One day, one boy from one school called Rugby School picked up the ball for the first time and ran with it. Everyone who saw him do this, got angry with him. But, later, the boy became a hero. He broke the rule and changed the game forever. That boy called William Ellis, broke that rule and changed that game forever.

Many who are under satanic rule shall break that rule and change their lives forever after reading this book, in Jesus' name.

# EFFECTS OF INHERITANCE

If you have been coming to our meetings for any length of time, you will have been hearing us saying that the sins of a person's ancestors or parents can affect a person's fortune. The Hebrews chapter 7 that we have read, just as it is positively applicable to Levi and Abraham, is also negatively applicable.

Levi was born many years after Abraham yet, we read that he paid tithes through Abraham. This means that, even though he was not born, he was already inside Abraham's loins.

Many people's fore-fathers have paid tithes to the devil, and have gotten implicated by that problem, yet the deed was done when they were inside their great-grand-fathers.

That is why a lot of people complain of not knowing what is happening to their lives.

In other words, since our great-great-grand-fathers paid the tithes, spiritually, there is a legal backing to the harassments that people receive. They sometimes wonder why, despite calling the name of Jesus, their problems never go away. The truth is that someone had paid the tithe to the devil which is now troubling them or had made a promise to the enemy. But one good news is this: Even if you are a lawful captive, Jesus sets unlawful captives free, you are sure to be set free.

In Isaiah 49:24 –26 we read:

Shall the prey be taken from the mighty, or the lawful captive delivered? [25]But thus saith the LORD, Even the captives of the mighty shall be taken away, and the prey of the terrible shall be delivered: for I will contend with him that contendeth with thee, and I will save thy children. [26]And I will feed them that oppress thee with their own flesh; and they shall be drunken with their own blood, as with sweet wine: and all flesh shall know that I the LORD *am* thy Saviour and thy Redeemer, the mighty One of Jacob.

# THINGS THAT AFFECT ONE'S LIFE

### ➡ *The Vessel of Birth*

A sister was rushed to one of our meetings. She hopelessly wanted to commit suicide. We asked her what the problem was and she said she had courted a man for fourteen years only for the man to turn up just three days to the wedding and say he was not going ahead with the whole thing. This put the sister in the middle of nowhere and all she felt she could do was to die.

We persuaded her to go through deliverance rather than kill herself. She countered our persuasion with the argument that what she believed was that once a person has repented and has given his life to Christ, he is already a delivered person. At any rate, she agreed to go through a deliverance session.

The time it takes for a person to get delivered varies from person to person. While some may require five days to get delivered, others might require just five minutes.

The sister came on a Wednesday. On Thursday, we never saw her. We sent somebody to fetch her but she was not at home. Later the sister fell ill and had to be rushed to the Hospital. Still, people went to pray for her there.

[229]

Not quite five minutes after the prayer warriors left her, the mother came to the hospital and mocked the sister's efforts at getting married. She vowed the sister would never get married as her present sickness was one of the ploys she had employed to prevent her from getting married.

Now, as prayer was going on one day, the Lord said the sister had been delivered. She was discharged from the hospital eventually, after which she returned to our church to continue her deliverance.

On that same day, a message came that we should go to the same hospital to attend to someone who needed our attention. When we got there, we met the mother. Amazingly, when she got there, the sister was lying on the only available bed in the ward which incidentally was the bed used by the sister. At that particular place and time, the sister's illness was transferred onto the wicked woman.

### ➥ The Place of One's Birth

What we have just discussed concerns somebody's parents. But that is not the only thing. The place of one's birth can equally affect one's life, apart from the vessel of birth. For example, we read in Jeremiah 16: 1-4 that:

The word of the LORD came also unto me, saying, [2]Thou shalt not take thee a wife, neither shalt thou have sons or daughters in this place.

## Your Foundation and Your Destiny

³For thus saith the LORD concerning the sons and concerning the daughters that are born in this place, and concerning their mothers that bare them, and concerning their fathers that begat them in this land; ⁴They shall die of grievous deaths; they shall not be lamented; neither shall they be buried; *but* they shall be as dung upon the face of the earth: and they shall be consumed by the sword, and by famine; and their carcases shall be meat for the fowls of heaven, and for the beasts of the earth.

Jeremiah wanted a wife. Surely, his eyes must have caught some beautiful ladies in that land whom he would have loved to take as wife. And everything about the girl seemed satisfactory and perfect, with the right character, godliness, good training, the right height but, just as Jeremiah wanted to proceed, God intercepted him.

Certainly, as a man of God, Jeremiah would have expected God to explain why he could not have the woman after his heart for wife. And God seemed to have answered Jeremiah in the above passage: there was a problem with the girl's parentage and the land of her birth upon which there was a curse.

Verse 11 of the same passage tells us further:

Then shalt thou say unto them, Because your fathers have forsaken me, saith the LORD, and have walked after other gods, and have served them, and have worshipped them, and have forsaken me, and have not kept my law;

[231]

This gives us the nature of the curse on that land because of idolatry. It says anyone born in that land would not live long and would, in fact, die a grievous death. None of them would die a natural death; everyone who died would be killed by another, and that if Jeremiah should marry from such a place, and give birth to children through someone from that land, the same curse would affect them.

This was what God was telling Jeremiah. This mean that the place of birth has an effect on the future and the fortune of a person.

The issue of cursed places can be seen all over our nation Sometimes, people have a peculiar problem common to al of them from a particular place – poverty, sickness, suicide

In some places, people can only progress when they don' reside in their place of birth. If they should go there that would be their waterloo, all because of things like this.

There are some places where, even when the most successful businessmen get there, they will cease t progress for as long as they remain there. But immediate they move elsewhere, they will begin to prosper again.

Likewise, there are some houses where a person neve prospers until he leaves there, because the foundation c that place is already polluted.

I remember the testimony of a brother who lived in a block of flats. He was the last person to move in there. He moved in with two Mercedes Benz cars. But by the time he spent six months there, he started borrowing money to survive.

Then, one day, after hearing a message, his spiritual brain began to work. He took a look at the other tenants and saw that all of them had cars that were not working. What could be happening? He began to pray. During his prayer, the Lord led him to see a well in the compound. When the brother took a look inside the well he could see something in there.

After allowing everyone to go to work the next day, the brother called a labourer and asked him to siphon all the water inside the well. After this was done, a tortoise was found at the bed of the well with a red cloth tied round it. When the brother brought out the tortoise and untied the red cloth wound around it, he discovered that the names of all the tenants were written on the red cloth. The brother's name was the last one on the list. Obviously, something was wrong with that place.

When the other tenants returned, the brother told the whole story to all other tenants, but only one of them was born again. The man understood the matter readily and began looking for an alternative accommodation. The remaining four tenants, being academics, dismissed the whole thing as superstition.

When the two Christian brothers moved out of the bewitched premises, they began to prosper once again. The other academic tenants remained there, and they remained poor.

What I am saying is this: You could have a very good business but if it is established on a cursed land, nothing good will happen there. If you read Daniel chapter 10, you will find that there are spirits over territories and places; every geographical area has its own controllers.

For example, as one goes from one place to another, one will see certain spirits dominating the people living in a particular area.

An example of this is the deliverance we did, not long ago for people from riverine areas governed by marine spirits that make girls from there morally loose. There, erratic marriages, single parenthood and infidelity are the order of the day.

People from different parts of the world are possessed by different spirits, depending on the type of spirit that is operating in that abode.

When people from these different places come together for marriage, their offspring automatically inherit the traits, unless they are born again.

There is an example of this in the Bible. When Daniel was in the land of bondage, in Babylon, Angel Michael who was the prince of their people was there with Daniel.

It was probably the same Michael that led them out of Egypt. And right there in Babylon the same Angel went to be with Daniel, not caring whether he was in bondage.

I also remember that when the Israelites were in Egypt, which was not their place, as they went out, something of Egypt followed them. It took them a day to get out of the land of Egypt, but it took thirty years to get the land of Egypt out of their lives. So the place of birth is of great importance.

For example, maybe where you were born, witches fly openly in day light. This may make you a blind witch. A man may be away from home and still be under the remote controlling powers of his place of birth. This makes it imperative for you to pray really hard.

➥ *The Time of Birth*

Apart from the vessel of birth, the place of birth, as well as the time of birth can also be a problem, especially where people believe in astrology. But if you are a Christian, your place of birth changes immediately you were born again under the star of Bethlehem, and not just any star.

Certainly, you would not group your birth under Scorpion, or Cancer, the spirits of which have a bearing on the lives of those who believe in them.

### ➤ Your Immediate Environment

The environment you were born or raised in goes a long way in controlling your destiny. Scientific research has proved that the environment of a baby and his mother affects them. The mother's diet, the kind of music she listens to and the kind of words she hears will definitely affect her child. If a baby is born by a mother who is addicted to smoking and drinking, such a child will be affected.

Therefore, you must specifically pray against problems emanating from your environment.

I am aware of the fact that a lot of people were born into traditional maternity homes or hospitals that are dedicated to the devil. Such people need to carry out serious prayer programmes until they are completely set free.

## Your Foundation and Your Destiny

What a baby is subjected to in the womb and the circumstances surrounding his birth, will determine the destiny of the baby.

For example, the destiny of an unwanted child will be affected negatively. If a couple has already had six children and another baby is conceived in the womb mistakenly, there may be a problem.

If such a child is born, he will grow up to struggle with the problems associated with amputated destiny. Such a child will grow up trying to please everyone around. He may grow up to be a 'yes man'.

Such children are generally apologetic and they suffer frequent illness. They even go ahead to reject any form of affection shown towards them.

When a child is conceived out of wedlock, such a child is raised from a negative womb environment. By the time the child grows up, he may also become involved with polygamy. He would go into illicit relationships without any sense of shame.

Babies that are born by unmarried or teenage mothers would grow up with rebellious tendencies.

## Your Foundation and Your Destiny

If a couple is expecting a male child and a female child born, such a child will grow up with defeatist mind-set. Sh will grow up believing that everybody is against her.

When a child is raised in an atmosphere that characterised by hostilities and frequent squabbles, such child will become nervous, quarrelsome, fearful an hyperactive.

Any child born by a mother who happens to be a heav smoker will grow up to suffer from deep anxiety.

Again, if a child is born by a mother who is an alcoholi negative feelings will envelope the heart of the child.

For example, children that are born with the umbilic cord wrapped around their necks often develop thro: problems, speech impairment and may end up wit criminal tendencies.

At this point, I want you to take this important pray point.

*Every information about my life present on satan altars, be roasted, in the name of Jesus.*

# THE PROBLEMS OF A MAN

What I have explained so far is the key magnet keeping the spiritual problems of man in place. Until decisive prayers are done in this regard, modern methods will not help.

The circumstances surrounding your birth and the spiritual environment in which you have grown up are responsible for forty percent of the problems you find yourself in. These problems are knotty and fundamental. Unless you look into your background, you may continue to suffer the effect of this damaging chronic problems.

There is no way you can deal with this problem unless you can deal with any form of bondage that is associated with your foundation. Inability to deal with these problems has become responsible for the backwardness of the human race generally.

No wonder the Bible says,

Psalm 74:20: Have respect unto the covenant: for the dark places of the earth are full of the habitations of cruelty.

[239]

# THE POWERS AND WEAPONS THAT ARE FRUSTRATING THE HUMAN-RACE

This shows that wicked territorial spirits are very busy frustrating the human race. These are their weapons.

### ➥ Foundational Idolatry

Idol worship is the bane of the human race. God hates idolatry with perfect hatred. The Bible says:

Exodus 20:4-5: Thou shalt not make unto thee any graven image, or any likeness *of any thing* that *is* in heaven above, or that *is* in the earth beneath, or that *is* in the water under the earth: ⁵Thou shalt not bow down thyself to them, nor serve them: for I the LORD thy God *am* a jealous God, visiting the iniquity of the fathers upon the children unto the third and fourth *generation* of them that hate me;

God has made heavy and grievous pronouncements against all idol worshippers and their generations. Unfortunately, idol worship is still entrenched in the communal life of many people. This is the reason we have to take the gospel to the nooks and crannies of the world.

Idol worship has been dressed in a modern garb. In some parts of the world, airconditioned shrines are being built for idols. Many people are still living in the seventeenth century.

[240]

Since our fore-fathers have been worshipping idols, tell me what benefits have we derived? Nothing. Instead, we have continued to reap a harvest of bondage, slavery, untimely death, backwardness, failure at the edge of miracles, financial embarrassment and retrogression.

I pity those who are advocating for the return of the idolatrous practices of the past. Such people have labelled Christianity as the white-man's religion. They go about deceiving people by advocating for the return to the religion of our fore-fathers. These people live in air-conditioned houses. I wonder how many of them would agree to drink from worm-infested streams and live in mud houses with roofs made of thatched leaves.

Such people have been blindly deceived to go back to the practices of their fore-fathers.

Idolatry will always lead men and women into bondage, even if it is practised with the refinement of modernity.

### ➡ *Polygamy and Concubinage*

This is a major source of foundational bondage. Polygamy is more prevalent in the African communities than other countries of the world. Thus, many are operating under the anointing of Solomon, the man with a track record in polygamy. He had 700 wives and 300 concubines.

Polygamy provides a fertile ground for deep problems to thrive.

### ➤ *Familiar Spirits*

There are lots of strange children who are possessed by familiar spirit in many nursery, primary and secondary schools. Many innocent children and youngsters are loaded with familiar spirits. They perpetrate terrible havoc without giving anyone the impression that they are wicked satanic agents.

A nursing sister came to narrate her plight to me. She was attached to a popular secondary school in Lagos, Nigeria. Being one of the medical staff on a night shift charged with the responsibility of taking care of students who might have health problems, she thought it would be business as usual, nurses on night duty often sleep whenever there is no case to handle in the mini-clinic.

This Christian nursing sister was thinking of taking a nap when a young female student walked in without using the door. The unwanted visitor pointed straight at the nursing sister and declared,

"What have you come to do here? You had better be careful. Your predecessor stepped on our toes and we dealt with her. If you are not careful, we will deal with you too. Although, we are aware that you are fond of praying some dangerous prayers, we will teach you a lesson if you disturb us"

Before the sister could know what was happening, everything around her began to turn. She came to me the following day saying that she had decided to resign her appointment as a result of her frightening experience with the familiar spirit girl.

Familiar spirits litter our public and private schools. The innocent birthday parties that are done in schools have become avenues for recruiting new members. The cookies and confectionaries that are being served are instruments of extending the familiar spirit cult or society. That is why one can come across a student that was formally brilliant, becoming a dunce. Such transfer of virtue is made possible through birthday biscuits.

If you listen to the confessions of ex-familiar spirit members, you will discover that their best past time is the destruction of countless number of souls.

➡ *Territorial Bondage*

Territorial spirits take charge of communities, cities and nations. Thus, people from some localities operate under the umbrella of wicked territorial powers.

Territorial spirits are responsible for the problems of non-achievement, poverty, failure at the edge of success, marital turbulence, suicidal tendencies, ministerial failures and other terrible problems.

### ➡ *Blood Covenants*

Blood covenants lead to heavy foundational bondage. Many people's blood has been siphoned to evil altars through circumcisions, tribal marks and incisions. Most traditional or local circumcision experts are demonic. Those who make tribal marks on the face and other parts of the body use the same local knife from year to year. Thus, their circumcision knives have been converted to a mini-blood sucking altar.

In most parts of the world, particularly in Africa, there is hardly anyone whose foundation does not have a record of circumcision or incision.

Many people have formed secret blood covenants with their ancestors, through such traditional practices.

### ➡ *Land Covenants*

The land ownership system is fraught with dangers. Many of our ancestors have formed many deep covenants with lands. In Asian and African countries, pouring libations on the ground and performing some rituals in order to retain ownership of communal land are avenues for forming destructive land covenants. That is why many people keep on returning to their homestead in their dreams.

### ➧ Inherited Burdens and Curses

Many people carry burdens which they inherited from their ancestors. Such heavy burdens must be destroyed.

### ➧ Water Spirits

They always do everything in order to maintain and exercise dominion over their victims. What has the Bible got to say about these marine sprits?

Ezekiel 29:3-5: Speak, and say, Thus saith the Lord GOD; Behold, I am against thee, Pharaoh king of Egypt, the great dragon that lieth in the midst of his rivers, which hath said, My river is mine own, and I have made it for myself. ⁴But I will put hooks in thy jaws, and I will cause the fish of thy rivers to stick unto thy scales, and I will bring thee up out of the midst of thy rivers, and all the fish of thy rivers shall stick unto thy scales. ⁵And I will leave thee thrown into the wilderness, thee and all the fish of thy rivers: thou shalt fall upon the open fields; thou shalt not be brought together, nor gathered: I have given thee for meat to the beasts of the field and to the fowls of the heaven.

Here, Pharaoh was introduced as a water spirit. Many water spirits are active today. That is why people from riverine areas are of the world go through many complicated problems.

## ➡ *Evil Altars*

Many evil altars litter cities, towns, villages and country sides of the world. When we talk of evil altars, we are not only referring to shrines where we can find fetish objects dripping with blood or palm-oil, kola-nut, cowry shells or coins and other objects when you see such things at junctions or cross-roads, you are beholding an evil altar. Such altars are being created on daily basis. These have affected the destiny of man.

## ➡ *Polluted Thrones*

Many thrones are polluted in many countries of the world. Many thrones and seats of government have been covenanted to the devil. When the devil is controlling a nation, anyone who gets elected into public office there, will continue to mess things up.

## ➡ *Buried virtues*

Many people's virtues have been buried. Such virtues cannot come to the surface unless they are exhumed through the power of aggressive deliverance prayers.

Wicked satanic agents go into deep covenants with land demons, in order to bury people's virtues. Problems emanating from this wicked act require deep deliverance.

### ➥ *Spells and Jinxes*

People from all races of the world suffer terrible spells which they cast on themselves with reckless abandon.

### ➥ *The Spirit of Servant-hood*

Some nations of the world are suffering from this problem. This wicked spirit of servant-hood has been harassing many nations for a long time.

### ➥ *Manipulation of Dreams*

A lot of people have been caged through their dreams. A number of people are suffering from nightmarish dreams. Wicked satanic agents are busy converting many people's dreams to weapons of oppression.

### ➥ *Name Manipulation*

The names which many of us bear leave much to be desired. Many of our names bear negative testimonies to the power of terrible idols. I have come across people with names like darkness, dog, stone, death, etc.

A sister came to ask me what to do concerning her name. She told me that her name was Griffin and according to the dictionary, it means "A vulture with the face of a monkey" Don't laugh. Check up the meaning of your name.

[247]

### ➥ *Evil Spiritual Marriage*

The problem of spirit husband or wife has destroyed many lives. Whenever anyone is involved with a demonic or spiritual marriage, the physical marriage will experience turbulence.

For example, if a man is married in the spirit world, the spiritual partner will harass the living daylight out of the real earthly wife.

Again, if a woman has contracted marriage in the spirit world, her earthly husband would suffer serious attacks.

Someone came to me with a very serious problem. At that time, his third wife had just packed out of the matrimonial home. The man lamented bitterly, telling me that was how his first and second wives packed out at different times.

Each time he got married to a new wife, the wife would complain that she is being harassed in her dream by a particular woman. The harassment became so tough that all the women the man got married to ran out of the home in order to save their lives. This shows that spirit wives do not tolerate competition.

### ➥ *Household Wickedness*

This is a common parlance in spiritual warfare circles. Household wickedness is a wicked spirit. Having known the background of their victims, they launch virulent attacks against them. Since these enemies come from our own camps, they know the right strategies to use as well as the right weapons to make use of.

### ➥ *Destiny Converters*

There is a special demonic squad called destiny converters. Their main pre-occupation is to convert good destinies to bad ones.

### ➥ *Collective Captivity*

People who are raised in the same household or community, generally suffer the yoke of collective captivity. They share the same problems, travails and satanic attacks in common. Once collective captivity is in place nobody is exempted.

### ➥ *Demonic Consumption*

A lot of people have eaten at the altar of the devil in their bid to find solutions to life's problems. Even if you swallow anything in order to protect yourself, you will continue to experience serious problems until you vomit such demonic food.

### ➡ *Wastage*

This is a very serious problem. The spirit of wastage is very destructive. Whenever these powers are at work, they facilitate the destruction of lives, property, destiny, fortunes, good prospects and health. They ensure that what you labour to accumulate is wasted.

### ➡ *Incisions*

Incisions appear harmless, but they are deeply demonic. Any incision in your body is nothing but a satanic mark. You need to pray against the demonic influence of these evil marks. Until you do this, you will continue to struggle with problems that will defy solutions.

### ➡ *Sacrifice*

Anyone who has been involved with offering sacrifices to idols or demons should surrender himself for deliverance. If you had ever carried sacrifices for your parents, you have innocently placed yourself under a very heavy yoke. The dark power which you offered sacrifices to, years ago, will constantly pay you unexpected visits, since a link has been established between you and them.

### ➡ *Libations*

The act of pouring libations on the ground in honour of the gods of the land is an avenue for inviting satanic bondage. This is done during communal festivals, dedication of houses, cars and when foundation is laid for a new building.

Again, libations are poured during marriage ceremonies. These rituals attract the attention of powerful wicked demons.

### ➡ *The Act of Piercing the Nose and the Ear*

This is a common practice in many societies of the world. However, the act of piercing the ears and the nose is deeply rooted in idolatry.

### ➡ *The Demon of Poverty*

This is the chief demon working against the human race Poverty is not ordinary. There is a spirit behind it. How should someone labour like an elephant and eat like an ant? Of course, something is wrong somewhere.

### ➡ *Destructive Incantations*

This is a practice whereby the power of the spoken word is used negatively to destroy lives and properties. In those days, the use of incantations was restricted to fetish priests and hard-core satanic priests. Nowadays, incantations are being recited on the television.

## Your Foundation and Your Destiny

### ➡ Family and Environmental Strongman

Every family or community has an environmental strongman attached to it. This wicked personality ensures that everyone under his authority lives under perpetual bondage. The devil has strategically positioned the strongman in every nuclear family unit in order to destroy lives.

### ➡ Satanic Priests and Prophets

So-called prophets have cleverly combined fetish practices with elements of Christianity in order to destroy many lives. Before, the advent of Pentecostalism in some parts of the world, there was proliferation of 'white garment churches'. The prophets and prophetesses attached to these churches have planted evil seeds in the lives of many people.

### ➡ Placenta Manipulation

Many lives have been manipulated negatively through their placentas. The placentas of many people have been buried or kept in strange places. This has continued to be used by demonic agents to place many people under misery and woe.

## Your Foundation and Your Destiny

### ➥ Star Hunters

A lot of satanic agents are expert star manipulators in many nations of the world. People who would have achieved great things in life have failed woefully because their stars were caged at the time of their birth.

### ➥ Sand Operators

This may not be known to many people. A lot of people use the sand to divine the future and detect secret things. When satanic agents press the sand and mention the victims' names, the fates of such people are handed over to land demons.

### ➥ Evil Gates

A good number of towns or villages have gates or constructed entry points. These gates are manipulated by the devil and provide easy access to the lives of the inhabitants of the city.

### ➥ Demonic Cultural Festivals

In some nations of the world, particularly in Africa, promoters of African culture are still very busy canvassing for the revival of the tradition of their fathers. A lot of people travel home during traditional festive periods. Programmes like the new Yam festival and other festivals that are carried out from community to community have provided fertile grounds for satanic attacks.

### ➡ *Promoting the Inferior and Demoting the Superior*

This is one of the most serious problems associated with the human race. This evil exchange has led to the exaltation of nonentities and the pulling down of many people with exceptional talents and qualities.

### ➡ *Anti-maintenance Spirit*

If you have ever travelled to some parts of this world, you would have discovered that much premium is placed on maintenance of good amenities, utilities, gadgets and property. The story is different in Africa. People spend fortunes to acquire facilities or gadgets only to watch these things getting rotten without any form of maintenance culture. The anti- maintenance spirit is peculiar to the black race and thereby working against them.

### ➡ *Polluted wealth*

A local adage says, "The foundation of wealth stinks." The 'get-rich-quick' syndrome has led many to acquire wealth through ritual killing, occult practices and fetish manipulations. A lot of people in the world are spending blood money.

## Your Foundation and Your Destiny

### ➤ *Black against Black*

Again, this is a problem peculiar to Africans. Blacks are daggers drawn against one another. The number of black men that black men themselves have killed far surpasses the number killed by the whites during the days of colonialism and slave trade. It is unfortunate that blacks are their own worst enemies.

### ➤ *Consultation of Dark Spirit*

The desire to know what the future holds has pushed many people of the world to places where they have consulted wicked dark powers.

### ➤ *Eaters of Flesh and Drinkers of Blood*

This is the greatest problem bedevilling the African race. Blood-sucking witches and wizards have destroyed many lives. Parts of the body have been eaten, whole human beings have been swallowed alive .The Bible recognizes the activities of these wicked powers and prescribes the type of prayer point to use as weapon against them.

Psalm 27:2: When the wicked, *even* mine enemies and my foes, came upon me to eat up my flesh, they stumbled and fell.

These forty problems are kept in place through the place of birth as well as the environment where many people were raised.

# HOW THEN CAN WE DEAL WITH THESE PROBLEMS?

If you can take the following steps, you will experience total deliverance.

### ➤ *Total repentance*

If you are living in any known sin, if you do not repent, you will go about with partial deliverance.

### ➤ *Discernment*

Until you discern and know what to pray about, you may continue to suffer.

### ➤ *Persistence*

The power behind this problem is very stubborn and resilient. The devil will not give up easily. It requires constant bombardment to send the strangers out of their hiding places. Deal decisively until the fire power of your prayers weaken the enemy.

### ➤ *Violence*

The language of violence is the only language the devil understands and will flee from you. To resist the devil, you need a great deal of violence in your voice.

[256]

## Your Foundation and Your Destiny

The prayer session that is attached to this chapter is very unique. Your survival and total deliverance depend on them. Therefore, I counsel you to pray the way you have never done before.

Your level of victory and deliverance depends on it. Pray like a wounded lion and watch the devil panic and release whatever he has held unto in any department of your life.

This is your hour of deliverance.

# PRAYER POINTS

1. You spirit of _ _ _, (mention the name of your place of birth here) loose your hold upon my life in the name of Jesus.

2. Make these powerful declarations.

I break the stronghold of witchcraft and evil manipulation I command you to go down to the place which Jesus has provided for you, never to return anymore.

I bind and cast out any spirit of witchcraft in the name of Jesus. With the Sword of the Spirit, I root out every deep rooted problem.

I render null and void ungodly covenants, I render null and void every union agreement . I cut off all the powers feeding my problem, in the name of Jesus. I wipe out every evil decision about my life. I command any demonic bondage to break, in the name of Jesus.

3. I release myself from the consumption of every evil food, in the name of Jesus.

4. Heavenly surgeons, perform your surgical operation in my life, in the name of Jesus.

5. Every anointing of poverty, break, in the Jesus name .

6. Every idol from my place of origin, loose your hold upon my life, in the name of Jesus.

7. Every power planning evil for me, be exposed and disgraced, in the name of Jesus.

8. O Lord, wash my head with Your blood, in the name of Jesus.

9. Every destiny arrester from the womb, loose your hold, in the name of Jesus.

10. Every promise made by my parents on my behalf to any dark power, be broken, in the name of Jesus.

11. If I have walked into captivity with my own legs, O Lord, deliver me, in the name of Jesus.

12. Every placenta bondage, be dismantled, in the name of Jesus.

13. Every territorial curse, I revoke you, in the name of Jesus.